I0427797

CYBER INCIDENT RESPONSE: BRIDGING THE GAP BETWEEN CYBERSECURITY AND EMERGENCY MANAGEMENT

JOINT HEARING

BEFORE THE

SUBCOMMITTEE ON EMERGENCY PREPAREDNESS, RESPONSE, AND COMMUNICATIONS

AND THE

SUBCOMMITTEE ON CYBERSECURITY, INFRASTRUCTURE PROTECTION, AND SECURITY TECHNOLOGIES

OF THE

COMMITTEE ON HOMELAND SECURITY HOUSE OF REPRESENTATIVES

ONE HUNDRED THIRTEENTH CONGRESS

FIRST SESSION

OCTOBER 30, 2013

Serial No. 113–39

Printed for the use of the Committee on Homeland Security

Available via the World Wide Web: http://www.gpo.gov/fdsys/

U.S. GOVERNMENT PRINTING OFFICE

87–116 PDF   WASHINGTON : 2014

For sale by the Superintendent of Documents, U.S. Government Printing Office
Internet: bookstore.gpo.gov   Phone: toll free (866) 512–1800; DC area (202) 512–1800
Fax: (202) 512–2250   Mail: Stop SSOP, Washington, DC 20402–0001

COMMITTEE ON HOMELAND SECURITY

MICHAEL T. MCCAUL, Texas, *Chairman*

LAMAR SMITH, Texas
PETER T. KING, New York
MIKE ROGERS, Alabama
PAUL C. BROUN, Georgia
CANDICE S. MILLER, Michigan, *Vice Chair*
PATRICK MEEHAN, Pennsylvania
JEFF DUNCAN, South Carolina
TOM MARINO, Pennsylvania
JASON CHAFFETZ, Utah
STEVEN M. PALAZZO, Mississippi
LOU BARLETTA, Pennsylvania
CHRIS STEWART, Utah
RICHARD HUDSON, North Carolina
STEVE DAINES, Montana
SUSAN W. BROOKS, Indiana
SCOTT PERRY, Pennsylvania
MARK SANFORD, South Carolina

BENNIE G. THOMPSON, Mississippi
LORETTA SANCHEZ, California
SHEILA JACKSON LEE, Texas
YVETTE D. CLARKE, New York
BRIAN HIGGINS, New York
CEDRIC L. RICHMOND, Louisiana
WILLIAM R. KEATING, Massachusetts
RON BARBER, Arizona
DONALD M. PAYNE, JR., New Jersey
BETO O'ROURKE, Texas
TULSI GABBARD, Hawaii
FILEMON VELA, Texas
STEVEN A. HORSFORD, Nevada
ERIC SWALWELL, California

GREG HILL, *Chief of Staff*
MICHAEL GEFFROY, *Deputy Chief of Staff/Chief Counsel*
MICHAEL S. TWINCHEK, *Chief Clerk*
I. LANIER AVANT, *Minority Staff Director*

SUBCOMMITTEE ON EMERGENCY PREPAREDNESS, RESPONSE, AND COMMUNICATIONS

SUSAN W. BROOKS, Indiana, *Chairwoman*

PETER T. KING, New York
STEVEN M. PALAZZO, Mississippi, *Vice Chair*
SCOTT PERRY, Pennsylvania
MARK SANFORD, South Carolina
MICHAEL T. MCCAUL, Texas *(ex officio)*

DONALD M. PAYNE, JR., New Jersey
YVETTE D. CLARKE, New York
BRIAN HIGGINS, New York
BENNIE G. THOMPSON, Mississippi *(ex officio)*

ERIC B. HEIGHBERGER, *Subcommittee Staff Director*
DEBORAH JORDAN, *Subcommittee Clerk*

SUBCOMMITTEE ON CYBERSECURITY, INFRASTRUCTURE PROTECTION, AND SECURITY TECHNOLOGIES

PATRICK MEEHAN, Pennsylvania, *Chairman*

MIKE ROGERS, Alabama
TOM MARINO, Pennsylvania
JASON CHAFFETZ, Utah
STEVE DAINES, Montana
SCOTT PERRY, Pennsylvania, *Vice Chair*
MICHAEL T. MCCAUL, Texas *(ex officio)*

YVETTE D. CLARKE, New York
WILLIAM R. KEATING, Massachusetts
FILEMON VELA, Texas
STEVEN A. HORSFORD, Nevada
BENNIE G. THOMPSON, Mississippi *(ex officio)*

ALEX MANNING, *Subcommittee Staff Director*
DENNIS TERRY, *Subcommittee Clerk*

CONTENTS

IV

Appendix

CYBER INCIDENT RESPONSE: BRIDGING THE GAP BETWEEN CYBERSECURITY AND EMERGENCY MANAGEMENT

Wednesday, October 30, 2013

U.S. HOUSE OF REPRESENTATIVES,
COMMITTEE ON HOMELAND SECURITY,
SUBCOMMITTEE ON EMERGENCY PREPAREDNESS,
RESPONSE, AND COMMUNICATIONS, AND
SUBCOMMITTEE ON CYBERSECURITY, INFRASTRUCTURE
PROTECTION, AND SECURITY TECHNOLOGIES,
WASHINGTON, DC.

The subcommittees met, pursuant to call, at 10:07 a.m., in Room 311, Cannon House Office Building, Hon. Susan W. Brooks [Chairwoman of the Emergency Preparedness, Response, and Communications subcommittee] presiding.

Present from Subcommittee on Emergency Preparedness, Response, and Communications: Representatives Brooks, Palazzo, Payne, and Clarke.

Present from Subcommittee on Cybersecurity, Infrastructure Protection, and Security Technologies: Representatives Meehan, Clarke, and Horsford.

Mrs. BROOKS. The Subcommittees on Emergency Preparedness, Response, and Communications and Cybersecurity, Infrastructure Protection and Security Technologies will come to order.

I would like to welcome our witnesses, everyone in the audience, and those who are watching this webcast to our joint hearing today on Cyber Incident Response.

I would like to start out by thanking Chairman Meehan and Ranking Member Clarke for working with me and Ranking Member Payne, who we anticipate both of those Members will be here shortly, on this important issue.

I would like to thank our witnesses for their patience as we have worked to reschedule this hearing, in addition in the slight delay this morning.

I would also like to thank the staffs who have worked together in preparing us for this very important hearing this morning.

October is Cybersecurity Awareness Month, and I think it is so very important that we observe this month in part of our awareness because it must be our ability to not only protect our networks and our critical infrastructure from intrusions, but also, what is our ability to respond should an intrusion become successful? After all, we do know that the threat of a cyber attack is real and in a speech just prior to her resignation former Secretary of Homeland Security Janet Napolitano discussed that threat. She forecasted

(1)

that our country will face a major cyber event that will have a serious effect on our lives, our economy, and the everyday functioning of our society.

Now, earlier this past week National Geographic Channel aired a program entitled "American Blackout"—a program which I watched with some interest on Sunday evening. It explored the cascading effects of a Nation-wide 10-day power outage caused by a cyber attack. For the Members of the committee, if you have not seen that I strongly recommend that you watch this show.

The movie was eye-opening and quite scary and happened to be on a topic that I had discussed just recently with Hoosier Power Companies in my district just last month. The effects of the blackout depicted in this movie caused serious public health and public safety issues, including severely impacting the food and water supply; the availability of fuel, which we also saw during Hurricane Sandy, which just 1 year ago yesterday when that horrific hurricane came upon our shores; the ability of hospitals to function; the ability to access money from ATM machines or to use credit cards; and most importantly, the ability to enforce the law and maintain civil society.

Now, I agree with the former Secretary when she noted that we have made some great strides in addressing cyber threat, but clearly more work must be done and must be done quickly. This assessment that work remains was echoed at a hearing we held in the Emergency Preparedness Subcommittee last month.

The 2013 National Preparedness Report released by FEMA earlier this year again highlighted States' concerns about their own cybersecurity capabilities. The 2013 report noted gains in cybersecurity at the State level but that the States continue to report that cybersecurity is among the lowest of their capabilities. Let me repeat that: It is among the lowest of the States' capabilities.

At that hearing California's homeland security advisor, Mark Ghilarducci, noted that cybersecurity is an emerging and evolving threat that everybody is still grappling to get their arms around. He noted that the Federal Government's ability to provide guidance to States has been rather limited.

I agree this is not an easy task, but information sharing about the threat and actions to take before, during, and after a cyber attack is critical. I hope that Ms. Stempfley will tell us about the Department's efforts to share information with State and local authorities including emergency managers, fusion centers, and the private sector to help them work to address and elevate the importance of this evolving threat; and that I hope that our State and local witnesses will also discuss how they share information and coordinate with relevant officials in their States and localities and with the private sector, which, I must note, controls at least 85 percent of our Nation's critical infrastructure. We must ensure that this coordination is taking place now so we are prepared to respond to a cyber incident that will have physical consequences.

I am also interested in learning today how DHS, working with other Federal agencies and departments and exercise participants, is working to address the lessons that were learned in the National-level exercise exercised in 2012, which simulated a large-scale cyber attack.

Just as I have noted the challenges we face in addressing the cyber threat, we must also discuss the progress that is being made. In my own district I am proud to say that the Indianapolis division of Homeland Security has established a cyber defense force to improve the overall cybersecurity preparedness of the Indianapolis metropolitan area, and the State of Indiana has included cybersecurity in its threat and hazard identification and risk assessment, or in its own THIRA.

The National Emergency Management Association is working also with Texas A&M to develop cybersecurity awareness training programs for emergency managers. Fusion centers are also becoming much more engaged in cybersecurity.

States are also taking innovative steps to address the threat. For example, Michigan has established the role of a chief security officer, which has oversight of both cybersecurity and physical security.

The National Guard is becoming much more engaged in cybersecurity as well. In Maryland the Air National Guard's 175th Network Warfare Squadron is assisting with the development of State cybersecurity assessments and has worked with Maryland Emergency Management on cybersecurity exercises.

Next month the North American Electric Reliability Corporation, or NERC, will hold GridEx 2013, an exercise that will test the electricity subsector's readiness to respond to a cyber incident including physical consequences.

These are all critically important steps, but as I noted earlier, much work remains to ensure we are prepared to respond to a cyber attack.

Chairman McCaul and Chairman Meehan have been working to develop thoughtful, effective cybersecurity legislation this Congress. I am pleased the draft bill that that committee has worked on includes provisions addressing cyber incident response and it is my hope that today's hearing will help to further inform that committee's work.

Before I conclude, I would like to ask unanimous consent to include in the record a statement from the National Governors Association, which provides greater details on steps States are taking to enhance their cybersecurity posture.

[The information follows:]

STATEMENT OF NATIONAL GOVERNORS ASSOCIATION

OCTOBER 30, 2013

On behalf of the Nation's governors, thank you for the opportunity to comment on bridging the gap between cybersecurity and emergency management. Protecting the Nation from cyber threats and their potential consequences requires strong partnerships among all levels of government, law enforcement, the military, and the private sector. Over the past several years, Governors have been working to improve the cybersecurity posture of their States and to improve State-Federal coordination. Based on these efforts and States' interaction with the Federal Government, we are pleased to offer the recommendations below.

STATE EFFORTS TO ADDRESS CYBERSECURITY

Since the terrorist attacks of September 11, 2001, and Hurricane Katrina in 2005, National preparedness and response activities have emphasized a "whole community" approach. Despite this progress, State-Federal coordination efforts for cybersecurity are still in their early stages. In the absence of unified Federal guidance,

States are moving forward to develop methods, strategies, and partnerships to improve their cyber resiliency and strengthen capabilities to prepare for, respond to, and recover from potential cyber attacks.

Governors are leading efforts to expand collaboration and drive change at both the State and Federal level. This is taking place through initiatives such as the National Governors Association (NGA) Resource Center for State Cybersecurity and the Council of Governors. Through these collaborative forums, Governors have identified a number of areas where enhanced Federal support and engagement could further assist States in this National effort. For instance, the Federal Government should:

- Enhance Federal coordination and consultation with States and recognize that Governors have emergency powers and authorities that can benefit the Federal Government.
- Leverage all available resources, such as the National Guard, to support both Federal and State cybersecurity missions.
- Provide flexibility for State investments in cybersecurity through reform of Federal grant programs and support for innovative State solutions that leverage existing resources such as fusion centers.
- Clarify Federal statutes, roles, and authorities to address cyber incident response, taking into consideration the role of States and the impact on current State laws and regulations.
- Improve information sharing and State access to Federal cybersecurity resources, such as those for technical support, education, training, and exercises.

ENCOURAGING ACTION AND PROMOTING BEST PRACTICES

Governors' efforts are focused on the need to improve not just States' cybersecurity, but that of the Nation. To help Governors address this challenge, NGA formed the Resource Center for State Cybersecurity in 2012. The Resource Center, co-chaired by Maryland Governor Martin O'Malley and Michigan Governor Rick Snyder, brings together experts from key State and Federal agencies and the private sector to provide strategic and actionable recommendations Governors can use to develop and implement effective State cybersecurity policies and practices.

On September 26, 2013, the NGA released *Act and Adjust: A Call to Action for Governors for Cybersecurity,* a paper that provides strategic recommendations Governors can immediately adopt to improve their State's cybersecurity posture (attached). NGA also released an electronic dashboard designed to provide Governors with an overview of their State's cybersecurity environment and assist them in monitoring implementation of the paper's recommendations. The dashboard is currently being pilot tested in Maryland and Michigan in conjunction with the Multi-State Information Sharing & Analysis Center (MS–ISAC). Through the Resource Center, Governors are exploring other vital areas as well, including:

- The role of fusion centers in collecting and disseminating real-time information on cyber threats to State agencies and law enforcement;
- Enhancing the cybersecurity of energy systems and the electrical grid in coordination with utility commissions, owners, and operators at the State level; and
- Developing a trained and enduring cyber workforce within State government.

LEVERAGING RESOURCES GOVERNMENT-WIDE

Identifying innovative solutions to address cybersecurity and secure the Nation against the growing cyber threat requires engagement by senior leaders at all levels of government. In addition to their work within their respective States, Governors also have engaged directly with the Federal Government through the Council of Governors (Council). Currently co-chaired by Governor O'Malley and Iowa Governor Terry Branstad, the Council brings together 10 Governors and the Secretaries of Defense and Homeland Security to address issues regarding the National Guard and homeland defense.

Since it was formally established in 2010, the Council has served as a valuable forum to facilitate coordination between State and Federal military activities, such as a 2010 agreement establishing dual-status command authority during major disasters. This authority was employed during recent events such as Hurricane Sandy and the Colorado floods. The Council is now working to turn this commitment to collaboration into similar actions to address State-Federal coordination on cybersecurity and the development of National Guard cyber capabilities.

Governors firmly believe the Guard's unique status serving both Governors and the President and its access to civilian-acquired skillsets makes it an ideal and cost-effective resource to address our Nation's growing cyber vulnerabilities. With the flexibility to support both Federal and State-related cyber missions, the Guard can be a force multiplier in support of the Department of Defense, the Department of Homeland Security (DHS), the Federal Bureau of Investigation and States. While the National Guard's role in cybersecurity is still being deliberated, Guard cyber units across the country are already demonstrating their unique capabilities including:

- *Serving as a key coordinating hub between various stakeholder groups.*—Several National Guard cyber units are actively engaged with their Governor's office, State emergency management agencies, State Chief Information Officers and other State, local, and Federal officials in the development of State cyber incident response plans. Several States have also integrated Guard units within their fusion center.
- *Providing key support services in planning, testing, training, and exercises.*— Guard unit participation is continuing to grow in State and National-level cyber exercises such as Cyber Guard, Cyber Storm, and Cyber Shield. Several State Guard units also are providing risk assessment and vulnerability testing support to State agencies and local critical infrastructure owners and operators.
- *Providing a readily available and highly-trained workforce.*—National Guard cyber units include personnel from a significant number the Nation's top cybersecurity and information technology companies such as Microsoft, Cisco, Siemens, Intel, GE, Boeing, IBM, and Google. This access provides a unique opportunity to leverage and sustain "leading edge" civilian-acquired cyber skillsets not readily available or easily built from within the Federal Government.

Earlier this year, Governors secured the commitment of former U.S. Department of Homeland Security Secretary Janet Napolitano and departing U.S. Department of Defense Deputy Secretary Ash Carter to work with them to identify new opportunities to strengthen the State-Federal partnership on cybersecurity and to better leverage existing resources such as the National Guard. This work is on-going, and we look forward to providing the committee an update on our progress early next year.

OPPORTUNITIES FOR STATE-FEDERAL ENGAGEMENT

As the development of Federal legislation to address cybersecurity continues, Governors urge Congress to consider the following recommendations:

- *Ensure coordination and consultation with States.*—Like all disasters, response and recovery begins at the State and local level. Federal cyber incident response guidance such as the National Cyber Incident Response Plan (NCIRP) must not be developed using a Federal-centric approach, but must integrate key State officials and consider Governors' authorities throughout the process.
- *Promote the role of the National Guard to support both Federal and State cybersecurity missions.*—This includes ensuring that the National Guard is considered concurrently with active duty forces in any new cyber force structure developed by U.S. Cyber Command and the military services.
- *Support State investments in cybersecurity through reform of homeland security preparedness grants.*—In recent years, decreased funding levels across preparedness grant programs combined with their current rigid requirements has limited States' ability to address emerging threats, such as cybersecurity, or provide adequate support to fusion centers.
- *Address ambiguities with cyber incident response.*—This includes clarifying current statutory authorities governing disaster management, such as the Stafford Act and the Economy Act. Roles and responsibilities of the various Federal agencies with cybersecurity coordination and operational authority during an incident should be better-defined and corresponding guidance to State and local authorities (such as the NCIRP) should be updated accordingly.
- *Improve information sharing with States to provide real-time intelligence on threats.*—Improving existing information-sharing capabilities such as the MS–ISAC and State and local fusion centers can further support this effort. DHS also can provide more structured and coordinated access to Federal cybersecurity initiatives such as workforce and training programs, Federal cybersecurity exercises, and forums for public-private partnerships.

CYBERSECURITY IS A SHARED RESPONSIBILITY

Governors recognize the critical need to improve our Nation's cybersecurity posture. This is an immense challenge that requires an unprecedented level of coordination among all levels of government and the private sector. Governors are committed to addressing this challenge within their States and are actively seeking to partner with their Federal counterparts. As the committee continues to consider the legislative path forward for cybersecurity, NGA stands as a ready resource for innovative policy solutions that will both support Governors' efforts and enhance the State-Federal partnership to address our Nation's most pressing cybersecurity challenges.

ATTACHMENT.—NGA PAPER

ACT AND ADJUST: A CALL TO ACTION FOR GOVERNORS FOR CYBERSECURITY

September 2013, Thomas MacLellan, Division Director, Homeland Security & Public Safety Division, NGA Center for Best Practices

Cybersecurity remains one of the most significant challenges facing the Nation. Although implementing policies and practices that will make State systems and data more secure will be an iterative and lengthy process, Governors can take a number of actions immediately that will help detect and defend against cyber attacks occurring today and help deter future attacks.

Those actions include:
- Establishing a governance and authority structure for cybersecurity;
- Conducting risk assessments and allocating resources accordingly;
- Implementing continuous vulnerability assessments and threat mitigation practices;
- Ensuring that the State complies with current security methodologies and business disciplines in cybersecurity; and
- Creating a culture of risk awareness.

By implementing those recommendations immediately, Governors can greatly enhance States' cybersecurity posture.

Guiding Principles

This *Call to Action,* as well as the work of the NGA Resource Center for State Cybersecurity (Resource Center), is guided by a set of core principles:
- *Support Governors.*—The work of the Resource Center is singular in its focus on supporting Governors' efforts to improve cybersecurity. The Resource Center marks the first large-scale effort exclusively focused on the role of Governors in improving cybersecurity.
- *Be Actionable.*—The goal of the Resource Center is to provide to Governors recommendations and resources that promote actions that reduce risk.
- *Reduce Complexity.*—Cybersecurity policy is designed and implemented in a complex environment. The Resource Center aims to reduce that complexity by looking for common principles and practices that are effective in that environment.
- *Protect Privacy.*—The recommendations made through the Resource Center aim to both improve cybersecurity and protect the privacy, civil rights, and civil liberties of citizens.
- *Employ Technologically Neutral Solutions.*—The recommendations made through the Resource Center emphasize nonproprietary, open standards.
- *Focus on the State as Enterprise.*—The work of the Resource Center aims to improve Governors' understanding of the State as an enterprise including the interdependencies among State agencies; between the public and private sector; and regionally across State boundaries.
- *Promote Flexible Federalism.*—To the extent possible, the Resource Center emphasizes the benefits of and opportunities for flexibility within Federal programs to allow for tailored State solutions.
- *Rely on Evidence-Based Practices.*—The Resource Center makes recommendations that build on evidence-based practices.
- *Use and Generate Metrics.*—The Resource Center promotes recommendations that use dynamic performance metrics to manage and improve State processes and practices.
- *Promote the Use of Incentives.*—The Resource Center makes recommendations that promote the use of incentives to improve cybersecurity practices in a State.

Immediate Actions to Protect States

Domestic and international actors are launching a significant number of cyber attacks against States. Although many of the actions necessary to reduce the Nation's vulnerabilities to cyber attacks require long-term structural improvements and business redesign, Governors can take actions now that can immediately improve their State's cybersecurity posture. Implementation of the actions described below will help to ensure strong governance and oversight, a baseline of cybersecurity capabilities, and quicker identification of attacks and threats; it also will help to improve basic cybersecurity practices.

Establish a governance structure for cybersecurity.—Because State systems and networks are interconnected, developing a robust cybersecurity posture will require an enterprise-wide approach. To that end, Governors need to ensure that they have a strong State-wide governance structure with some degree of central authority that provides a framework to prepare for, respond to, and prevent cyber attacks. Several recent attacks reveal that States which fail to put in place a strong governance structure are at a distinct disadvantage.

For many States, chief information security officers (CISOs), who are responsible for developing and carrying out information technology (IT) security policies, have only limited responsibility and authority over State-wide cyber networks. CISOs can operate in federated or decentralized environments where technology and security resources are dispersed across various agencies and departments. In addition, the sharing of cyber threat information with the private sector and local governments is handled by State homeland security agencies, further complicating the overall cybersecurity governance structure.

According to a survey conducted by Deloitte for the National Association of State Chief Information Officers (NASCIO), 56 percent of State CISOs indicate that they have authority over only their executive branch agencies, departments, and offices.[1] Although most States have a CISO, if they do not have a visible agency-level security posture, they can encounter obstacles to implementing an effective cybersecurity program. Among the elements of an effective program are enforcement mechanisms to ensure compliance with security policies and audit findings. States without governance structures to build and operate effective programs will be limited in their ability to identify an on-going cyber attacks and respond in a coordinated way.

Governors can grant their chief information officers (CIOs) or CISOs the authority to develop and steer a coordinated governance structure (for example, a task force, commission, or advisory body) that can greatly improve coordination and awareness across agencies that operate State-wide cyber networks. Such an approach also helps enable the CIO or CISO to take actions to prevent or mitigate damage in the event of a cyber breach.

Michigan has created a centralized security department run by a chief security officer (CSO) that brings together both physical security and cybersecurity. Directors, managers, and employees within each agency coordinate through the centralized governance structure to focus on each agency's need for both physical security and cybersecurity. Governance of that type is especially important during an incident or a disaster. The approach allows the CSO and CIO to work closely to manage the State's cyber networks and infrastructure and to ensure that effective governance practices are in place.

Although a central authority is essential, it does not obviate the importance of collaboration among local governments, nongovernmental organizations, and the private sector. Those relationships are essential to understanding the culture, operations, and business practices of various agencies and organizations with cyber assets within the State. In Michigan, for example, in addition to dedicated and full-time State employees in the Office of Cybersecurity, a risk management team leverages many resources around the State to gather information and resolve an incident efficiently and effectively.

Minnesota is another example of a State that adopted a governance framework that stresses teamwork and communication between a centralized information technology organization and stakeholders. The State CIO works collaboratively with the Governor, the Technology Advisory Committee, and other agency leaders. Minnesota also has several governing bodies that have an agency CIO, providing a direct link to the State CIO and operational decisions made at the different agency team levels.[2]

Recognizing the need to foster collaboration at all levels of government and with the private sector, California recently created the California Cybersecurity Task Force. The task force focuses on sharing information to improve the security of Government and private-sector IT assets.[3]

Conduct risk assessments and allocate resources accordingly.—Governors and other key State actors need a comprehensive understanding of the risk and threat

---

[1] "State Governments at Risk: A Call for Collaboration and Compliance," Deloitte and the National Association of State Chief Information Officers, October 26, 2012, accessed March 10, 2013, *http://www.deloitte.com/assets/Dcom-UnitedStates/Local%20Assets/Documents/AERS/us_aers_nascio% 20Cybersecurity%20Study_10192012.pdf,* 10.

[2] "State of Minnesota IT Governance Framework," *http://mn.gov/oet/images/StateofMinnesotaITGovernanceFramework.pdf* (June 2012).

[3] "California Launches Cybersecurity Task Force," *http://www.govtech.com/security/California-Launches-Cybersecurity-Task-Force.html* (May 17, 2013).

landscape to make accurate and timely decisions when allocating scarce resources. Without a comprehensive understanding of the risks, including the interdependencies among critical assets, States are vulnerable to interruptions in business operations as well as financial and data losses. To gain this awareness, States must develop security strategies and business practices by conducting risk assessments that identify information assets, model different threats to those assets, and allow for planning to protect against those threats.[4]

In addition to establishing sound business practices and using existing resources, States also must conduct hands-on activities and exercises as a part of their assessments. Those practices include regular penetration testing and vulnerability scanning and should be referenced in security policies. States can take advantage of resources from Federal and private entities to conduct those activities. Once an independent State-wide assessment has been conducted, Governors can make necessary decisions on where scarce resources should be allocated to prevent the loss of essential information and resources and to protect critical infrastructure and assets. The initial assessment also will help determine the frequency of such assessments in the future, based on the risk profile of agencies. As an example, agencies with sensitive citizen data might require annual assessments and quarterly follow-up in their corrective action plan.

Additionally, Governors and their senior staff who have appropriate security clearances should receive regular classified cybersecurity threat briefings. The Department of Homeland Security (DHS) can assist States in planning these briefings.

Implement continuous vulnerability assessments and threat mitigation practices.— Consistently monitoring threats and vulnerabilities will help Governors proactively defend cyber networks. Every day, States are exposed to phishing scams, malware, denial-of-service attacks, and other common tactics employed by cyber attackers. Governors must ensure that mission-critical systems are equipped with technologies and have implemented business practices that will identify potential threats, track all stages of cyber attacks in real time, and offer mitigation techniques and options for any resulting loss or damage.

Maryland leverages the cybersecurity capabilities of the Maryland Air National Guard 175th Network Warfare Squadron to support its cybersecurity assessments. State agencies participate in collaborative web penetration training exercises with the Maryland Air Guard Squadron. The exercises that feature simulated attacks from malicious outsiders or insidious insiders are useful in evaluating the security of selected State websites and portals. Security issues uncovered through the penetration tests lead to technical and procedural countermeasures to reduce risks. The Guard also provides network vulnerability assessment services to various State agencies while, in return, it receives beneficial training for the squadron's members. A number of other States have similar practices in place.

The Multi-State Information Sharing and Analysis Center (MS–ISAC) has been designated by DHS as a key resource for cyber threat prevention, protection, response, and recovery for the Nation's State, local, territorial, and Tribal governments. Through its state-of-the-art Security Operations Center, available 24 hours a day, 7 days a week, the MS–ISAC serves as a central resource for situational awareness and incident response. The MS–ISAC also provides State, local, Tribal, and territorial governments with managed security services, which are outsourced security operations that include on-going monitoring of networks and firewalls for intrusions.

Another related resource available to State and local governments is DHS's newly-launched Continuous Diagnostics and Mitigation (CDM) program. The CDM program at the Federal level works by expanding deployment of automated network sensors that feed data about an agency's cybersecurity vulnerabilities into a continuously updated dashboard. To support States in improving their capabilities to prevent and detect intrusions, the CDM has a blanket purchasing agreement that reduces the cost to States of purchasing tools and services that enhance their cybersecurity. It is important to note that such purchases are most effective when coordinated with MS–ISAC's managed security services so as to maintain collective situational awareness across State and local governments.

Ensure that your State complies with current security methodologies and business disciplines in cybersecurity.—States can turn to two industry standards for a baseline of effective cybersecurity practices. First, the Council on CyberSecurity's *Critical Controls for Effective Cyber Defense* is an industry standard that provides States with a security framework that can strengthen their cyber defenses and ultimately protect information, infrastructure, and critical assets. Compliance with that stand-

---

[4] "5 Steps to Cybersecurity Risk Assessment" *http://www.govtech.com/security/5-Steps-to-Cyber-Security.html?page=1* (June 24, 2010).

ard will provide a baseline of defense, deter a significant number of attacks, and help minimize compromises, recovery, and costs. The controls are based upon five guiding principles: Using evidence-based practices to build effective defenses, assigning priorities risk reduction and protection actions, establishing a common language that measures the effectiveness of security, continuous monitoring, and automating defenses.[5] The controls also identify key network components and how to secure them.

The second standard is the Information Technology Infrastructure Library (ITIL). An ITIL is a set of practices for information technology service management (ITSM) that are designed to align information technology (IT) with core business requirements. The latest editions of ITIL, which were published in July 2011, form the core guidance of best management practices and can greatly strengthen States' IT practices. The ITIL has been adopted by companies in many private-sector industries, including banking, retail services, technology, and entertainment. For States, an ITIL will help ensure that States' IT assets correlate with their critical assets.[6]

Create a culture of risk awareness.—The best firewalls and most advanced antivirus software cannot deter a cyber attack if the individuals using a network are either careless or inattentive to basic security practices. The strongest door and most secure lock will not keep a burglar out if the door is left open or unlocked.

Governors have the opportunity to promote a culture of cybersecurity awareness that will help to minimize the likelihood of a successful cyber attack. Building a strong cybersecurity culture means making individuals aware of the many risks and on-going threats facing their networks. Those individuals must understand the potential negative implications of their activities or inattentiveness. To develop a strong cybersecurity culture, focus should be put on increasing awareness, setting appropriate expectations, and influencing day-to-day security practices of end-users. Awareness can be created by including relevant training and content in the orientation process of new staff as well as annual review of current staff. Expectations about users' behaviors can also be set by adding cybersecurity components to job responsibilities.

However, creating a culture of awareness will be an on-going process that will require constant attention and on-going training. Governors have the opportunity to use the bully pulpit to make cybersecurity the responsibility of all, including ordinary citizens. In Delaware, State employees conduct cybersecurity presentations for elementary school students to reinforce the importance of internet safety practices. The State also hosts video and poster contests that encourage the public to create materials that promote cybersecurity awareness.[7]

Effective awareness training and education for end-users is recognized as the single most effective factor in preventing security breaches and data losses. States such as Michigan have launched security awareness training for all State employees and have posted on-line guides that are available to the public with the goal of reducing risk.[8] More than 50,000 users and partners are currently enrolled in Michigan's training program, an on-line interactive program consisting of a dozen 10-minute lessons. Other organizations, such as the MS–ISAC, also offer training resources that are readily available on-line.

Michigan also has recently launched a research, test, training, and evaluation facility for cybersecurity and cyberdefense. In partnership with State universities, the private sector, and State and local governments, Merit Network Inc., a 501(c)(3) nonprofit organization, built and developed the state-of-the-art center to further advance cybersecurity training in Michigan. A wide variety of course offerings includes certifications in incident handling, disaster recovery, forensics, and wireless security. Dozens of technical staff have already completed training and received certifications.

In addition to offering training, States like Maryland conduct table-top exercises to raise the awareness and response capabilities of key State actors. Maryland, through the State's Emergency Management Administration (MEMA), facilitated an initial cabinet-level table-top exercise in which cybersecurity and continuity of operations awareness and readiness were assessed. In addition to MEMA, DHS and the National Security Agency Cyber Command assisted in hosting this exercise.

---

[5] "CSIS: 20 Critical Security Controls," *http://www.sans.org/critical-security-controls/guidelines.php.*

[6] "ITIL: The Basics," *http://www.best-management-practice.com/gempdf/ITIL_The_Basics.pdf.*

[7] See *http://www.dti.delaware.gov/information/cybersecurity.shtml.*

[8] See State of Michigan Security Office website.

The Path Forward

The actions described above are a first step for Governors to improve cybersecurity for State-owned and -operated systems. However, a secure cybersecurity fabric will require an enterprise-wide approach that includes coordination and partnerships with critical infrastructure owners and operators, private industry, and the public.

Over the course of the next year, the NGA Resource Center for State Cybersecurity will issue a series of reports focusing on critical areas for mid- to long-term actions Governors can take to strengthen their States' cyber posture. Those areas include improving coordination between State and Federal governments, leveraging State fusion centers to respond to cyber threats, enhancing the cybersecurity of critical energy systems and infrastructure, and developing a skilled cybersecurity workforce.

In addition to the work of the Resource Center, NGA also is leading efforts through the Council of Governors to collaborate with the Departments of Defense and Homeland Security on how the National Guard could be used to better protect both State and Federal networks. The National Guard's unique role serving Governors and the President, combined with its ability to attract and retain individuals who have full-time employment in IT and related fields, make it an ideal solution to help address the shortage of highly-skilled personnel necessary to protect critical networks and systems.

Across the country, several States have established National Guard cyber capabilities that are closely aligned with civilian agencies and coordinate regularly with public utility commissions, owners and operators of critical infrastructure, and other public and private-sector partners.

The NGA Resource Center for State Cybersecurity is made possible through the generous support from our grant makers, including the American Gas Association, Citi, Deloitte, Edison Electric Institute, Good Technology, Hewlett-Packard, IBM, Northrop Grumman, Nuclear Energy Institute, Symantec, and VMware.

Mrs. BROOKS. With that, I look forward to hearing from our distinguished panel of witnesses.

The Chairwoman now will recognize the gentlelady from New York, Ms. Clarke, for any opening statement she may have.

Ms. CLARKE. I thank Chairwoman Brooks and Ranking Member Payne as well as Chairman Meehan for holding today's joint subcommittee hearing.

We all know that cybersecurity is a matter of National, economic, and societal importance. Present-day attacks on the Nation's computer systems do not simply damage an isolated machine or disrupt a single enterprise system, but current attacks target infrastructure that is integral to the economy, National defense, and daily life.

Computer networks have joined food, water, transportation, and energy as critical resources for the functioning of the National economy. When one of these key cyber infrastructure systems is attacked, the same consequences exist for a natural disaster or terrorist attack.

National or local resources must be deployed. Decisions are made to determine where to deploy resources. The question is: Who makes these decisions?

The data required to make and monitor the decisions and the location of available knowledge to drive them may sometimes be unknown, unavailable, or both. Indeed, computer networks are the central nervous system of our National infrastructure and the backbone of emergency management is a robust cyber infrastructure. These systems enable emergency management agencies to implement comprehensive approaches to natural disasters, terrorist attacks, and law enforcement issues.

Mr. Payne has introduced a bill, the SMART Grid Study Act, that will give a fuller picture of the smart grid's role and our reliance on it, especially during an event where emergency management response is key to our resilience. I am glad to see the strong support that the National Electrical Manufacturers have given this bill and I especially look forward to their testimony today.

There is a general lack of understanding about how to describe and assess the complex and dynamic nature of emergency management tasks in relation to cybersecurity concerns. There are many issues involving knowledge integration and how to help managers improve emergency management task performance.

Ever since the first computer virus hit the internet it has been apparent that attacks can spread rapidly. Just as society has benefited from the nearly infinite connections of devices and people through the U.S. cyber infrastructure, so has malicious parties with the intent of taking advantage of this connectivity to launch destructive attacks.

We must find a way to develop tools that we can use to improve emergency management successes through effective handling, cyber complexity, cyber knowledge, and cyber integration at the ground level of our first responders.

Madam Chairwoman, I look forward to today's testimony and I yield back.

[The statement of Ranking Member Clarke follows:]

STATEMENT OF RANKING MEMBER YVETTE D. CLARKE

We all know that cybersecurity is a matter of National, economic, and societal importance. Present-day attacks on the Nation's computer systems do not simply damage an isolated machine or disrupt a single enterprise system, but current attacks target infrastructure that is integral to the economy, National defense, and daily life.

Computer networks have joined food, water, transportation, and energy as critical resources for the functioning of the National economy. When one of these key cyber infrastructure systems is attacked, the same consequences exist for a natural disaster or terrorist attack.

National or local resources must be deployed. Decisions are made to determine where to deploy resources. The question is: Who makes these decisions? The data required to make and monitor the decisions, and the location of available knowledge to drive them may sometimes be unknown, unavailable, or both.

Indeed, computer networks are the "central nervous system" of our National infrastructure, and the backbone of emergency management is a robust cyber infrastructure. These systems enable emergency management agencies to implement comprehensive approaches to natural disasters, terrorist attacks, and law enforcement issues.

Mr. Payne has introduced a bill, the Smart Grid Study Act, that will give a fuller picture of the smart grid's role and our reliance on it, especially during an event where emergency management response is the key to our resilience. I'm glad to see the strong support that the National Electrical Manufacturers have given this bill, and I especially look forward to their testimony today.

There is a general lack of understanding about how to describe and assess the complex and dynamic nature of emergency management tasks in relation to cybersecurity concerns. And there are many issues involving knowledge integration and how it helps managers improve emergency management task performance. Ever since the first computer virus hit the internet, it has been apparent that attacks can spread rapidly.

Just as society has benefited from the nearly infinite connections of devices and people through the U.S. cyber infrastructure, so have malicious parties with the intent of taking advantage of this connectivity to launch destructive attacks.

We must find a way to develop tools that we can use to improve Emergency Management successes through effectively handling cyber complexity, cyber knowledge, and cyber integration at the ground level for our first responders.

Mrs. BROOKS. Thank you.

I thank the Ranking Member of the Subcommittee on Cybersecurity, Infrastructure Protection, and Security Technologies and I now turn to the Ranking Member for the Emergency Preparedness, Response, and Communications, the gentleman from New Jersey, Mr. Payne, for any opening statements.

Mr. PAYNE. Thank you, Madam Chairwoman. Let me apologize for my tardiness, but Amtrak didn't cooperate this morning, so I apologize for that.

I would like to thank Chairwoman Brooks and Chairman Meehan for calling this hearing today.

Yesterday marked the 1-year anniversary of Super Storm Sandy, which devastated communities all along the Eastern Coast, especially in my home State of New Jersey. Although the people of New Jersey, with a lot of help from the Federal Government, have begun the long effort to rebuild what was lost, much work remains. I know that I am not alone when I say that the people affected by Hurricane Sandy can be sure that members of this panel will continue to work to make sure that the communities are rebuilt and the lessons learned are incorporated into future disaster plans.

With that, I will turn to the topic of today's hearing, responding to cyber attack. Last month the Subcommittee on Emergency Preparedness, Response, and Communications held a hearing reviewing the findings of the Federal Emergency Management Agency's 2013 National Preparedness Report. For the second year in a row, States indicated that of the 31 core capabilities, cybersecurity is one of the capabilities about which they are least confident.

The threats posed by a cyber attack are not new, but the impact of a cyber attack becomes more grave as every aspect of Government and the private sector become more reliant on cyber technologies. For example, communications essential to an effective emergency response, from the emergency alert system to E–911 and eventually FirstNet, all are vulnerable to cyber attack. The data networks and computer systems used to coordinate an efficient response to ensure that adequate resources are deployed to the appropriate locations are similarly vulnerable to a cyber breach.

A cyber attack on any of these systems could severely undercut Federal, State, and local abilities to respond to disasters effectively. Moreover, we have seen a significant increase in cyber threats to our critical infrastructure.

We know that disasters like Super Storm Sandy can wreak havoc on our power systems but rarely consider the harm that a malicious cyber attack could do to our electrical grid. Accordingly, I have introduced the SMART Grid Study Act, which will provide a comprehensive assessment of actions necessary to expand and strengthen the capabilities of our electrical power systems to prepare for and respond to, mitigate, and recover from a natural disaster or cyber attack to the electric grid. My legislation will go a long way to provide sector-specific awareness of cyber vulnerabilities and how to address them.

We must help State governments undertake similar efforts to understand the cyber threats posed to their networks and how to address them. It is no secret that a lack of funding has contributed to the lack of confidence States have in their cybersecurity capabilities. I would be interested in learning how cuts to homeland security grant funding since 2011 has affected States' cybersecurity efforts.

I have also heard that States have struggled to implement governing structure for cybersecurity and that finding a workforce with the appropriate training has proven difficult. So I would be interested to learn how the Department of Homeland Security is helping States identify best practices for an effective cybersecurity governance structure and improve training for State cybersecurity workforces.

I look forward to learning more about how State emergency managers are working with State chief information officers to understand the role each play in responding to a cyber incident.

I want to thank the witnesses for being here today and I look forward to their testimony.

Madam Chairwoman, I yield back the balance of my time.

[The statement of Ranking Member Payne follows:]

STATEMENT OF RANKING MEMBER DONALD M. PAYNE, JR.

OCTOBER 30, 2013

Yesterday marked the 1-year anniversary of Super Storm Sandy, which devastated communities all along the East Coast, and especially in my home State of New Jersey. Although the people of New Jersey—with a lot of help from the Federal Government—have begun the long effort to rebuild what was lost, much work remains.

I know I am not alone when I say that the people affected by Hurricane Sandy can be sure that members of this panel will continue to work to make sure that the communities are rebuilt and the lessons learned are incorporated into future disaster plans.

With that, I will turn to the topic of today's hearing: Responding to a cyber attack. Last month, the Subcommittee on Emergency Preparedness, Response, and Communications held a hearing reviewing the findings of the Federal Emergency Management Agency's 2013 National Preparedness Report. For the second year in a row, States indicated that—of the 31 core capabilities—cybersecurity is one of the capabilities about which they are least confident.

The threats posed by a cyber attack are not new. But the impact of a cyber attack becomes more grave as every aspect of Government and the private sector become more reliant on cyber technologies. For example, communications essential to an effective emergency response, from the Emergency Alert System, to E9–1–1, and eventually FirstNet, are all vulnerable to a cyber attack.

The data networks and computer systems used to coordinate an efficient response and ensure that adequate resources are deployed to the appropriate location are similarly vulnerable to a cyber breach. A cyber attack on any of these systems could severely undercut Federal, State, and local abilities to respond to disasters effectively.

Moreover, we have seen a significant increase in cyber threats to our critical infrastructure. We know that disasters like Super Storm Sandy can wreak havoc on our power systems but we rarely consider the harm that a malicious cyber attack could do to our electric grid.

Accordingly, I have introduced the SMART Grid Act, which would provide for a comprehensive assessment of actions necessary to expand and strengthen the capabilities of the electrical power system to prepare for, respond to, mitigate, and recover from a natural disaster or cyber attack to the electric grid.

My legislation will go a long way to provide sector-specific awareness of cyber vulnerabilities and how to address them. We must help State governments undertake similar efforts to understand the cyber threats posed to their networks and how to address them. It is no secret that a lack of funding has contributed to the lack of confidence States have in their cybersecurity capabilities.

I will be interested in learning how cuts to Homeland Security Grant funding since 2011 have affected State cybersecurity efforts. I have also heard that States have struggled to implement a governance structure for cybersecurity and that finding a workforce with the appropriate training has proven difficult.

So I will be interested to learn how the Department of Homeland Security is helping States identify best practices for an effective cybersecurity governance structure and improve training for State cybersecurity workforces. I look forward to learning more about how State Emergency Managers are working with State Chief Information Officers to understand the role each play in responding to a cyber incident.

Mrs. BROOKS. Thank you.

Other Members of the subcommittee are reminded that opening statements may be submitted for the record.

[The statement of Ranking Member Thompson follows:]

STATEMENT OF RANKING MEMBER BENNIE G. THOMPSON

OCTOBER 30, 2013

In 2010, former White House Counterterrorism Advisor Richard Clarke stated that this country's lack of preparation for a cyber attack could lead to a breakdown in our critical infrastructure system that would be like an "electronic Pearl Harbor." While some may consider his assessment a bit exaggerated, I think we would do well to remember it as we begin today's hearing.

We should also recall that in the 112th Congress, this committee marked up cybersecurity legislation. Unfortunately, the Republican leadership of the House did not allow that legislation to come to the floor of the House. In January, the President issued an Executive Order requiring certain basic steps that will improve this Nation's ability to protect and defend against cyber attacks.

While I applaud the President's efforts, I must point out that an Executive Order cannot expand existing legal authorities. In May of this year, the Department of Homeland Security testified before this committee that the "United States confronts a dangerous combination of known and unknown vulnerabilities in cyberspace." DHS also told us the Department processed approximately 190,000 cyber incidents involving Federal agencies, critical infrastructure, and the Department's industry partners—a 68 percent increase from 2011.

Mr. Chairman, I think that we should all have concern about cyber attacks on critical infrastructure—especially attacks that could disable the electric grid. For most of us, spending a day or two without electricity is an inconvenience. For others, it can be a matter of life or death. That is why I am pleased that Rep. Payne, Jr. introduced H.R. 2962, the SMART Grid Study Act. If enacted, the bill will require a comprehensive study to examine the construction, job creation, energy savings, and environmental protections associated with fully upgrading to a SMART Grid System. The information gathered in the study may help us reduce the frequency and severity of outages during disaster events. I urge my colleagues to support this bill.

Still, there is more to be done. We cannot begin to address the current threats or anticipate future vulnerabilities if we have not invested in the kind of education and training necessary to develop the next generation of cyber professionals. Federal, State, and local governments and the private sector are each vulnerable to cyber attacks. While the threats from and sophistication of hackers continues to grow, initiatives to address this mutual vulnerability must be comprehensive and coordinated. This country's history has repeatedly shown that a shared commitment to a common goal is necessary to achieve progress—from bringing electricity to the Nation to walking on the moon. Today, the same kind of commitment and collaboration is necessary to address the cyber threat.

Like every previous movement that resulted in progress, this first step must be education. That is why I am pleased that yesterday, this committee marked up Rep. Clarke's bill, H.R. 3107, the Homeland Security Cybersecurity Boots-on-the-Ground Act. This bill will help foster the development of a National security workforce capable of meeting current and future cybersecurity challenges, and it will outline how DHS can improve its recruitment and retention of cybersecurity professionals.

Mr. Chairman, I urge this committee to continue to put forward the kind of legislation that will help this Nation resolve our known vulnerabilities. More than any other committee, we must be on the forefront of proposing innovations and pushing forward common-sense solutions.

Mrs. BROOKS. We are pleased to have a very distinguished panel before us today on this important topic. So with that, I will begin the introductions of our panelists.

Ms. Bobbie Stempfley is the acting assistant secretary of the Office of Cybersecurity and Communications, where she plays a leading role in developing the strategic direction for CS&C and its five divisions. Ms. Stempfley previously served as the deputy assistant secretary for CS&C and as director of the National Cybersecurity Division, a legacy CS&C division. Prior to her work at CS&S, Ms. Stempfley served as the chief information officer for the Defense Information Systems Agency.

Next on our panel is Mr. Charley English, who was appointed director of the Georgia Emergency Management Agency/Homeland Security in February of 2006. He has served in the agency since 1996. He began his career in public service as a local police officer in 1980.

Other current responsibilities include serving as the president of the national Emergency Management Association, chair of the Governor's Commission on 9–1–1 Modernization, and State point of contact for the Nation-wide Public Safety Broadband Network. He earned a master's degree in homeland defense and security from the Naval Postgraduate School in 2004.

I now will yield to the gentleman from Mississippi, Ranking Member of our subcommittee, or I am sorry, vice chair of our subcommittee, Mr. Palazzo, to introduce our next witness.

Mr. PALAZZO. Thank you, Madam Chairwoman.

It is my pleasure to introduce Dr. Craig Orgeron. Dr. Orgeron is the chief information officer and executive director of the State of Mississippi's Department of Information Technology Services. He also has the honor of serving as the president of the National Association of State Chief Information Officers.

Dr. Orgeron has over 24 years of information technology experience in both the private sector and the Federal and State level of the public sector. He began his career as a communications computer systems officer in the United States Air Force, serving from 1988 to 1992.

Dr. Orgeron holds a bachelor's degree in management information systems, a master's degree and a doctorate in public policy and administration from Mississippi State University. Dr. Orgeron is a certified public manager and a graduate of the John C. Stennis State Executive Development Institute as well as the Institute of International Digital Government Research and the Harvard University John F. Kennedy School of Government executive education series "Leadership for a Networked World."

Thank you, Dr. Orgeron, for being here today, and I look forward to hearing your testimony.

I yield back.

Mrs. BROOKS. Thank you.

Next up is Mr. Mike Sena, who is the director of the Northern California Regional Intelligence Center and serves as president of the National Fusion Center Association. He has served in law enforcement for nearly 20 years, including the California Bureau of Investigation Intelligence, the California Bureau of Narcotics Enforcement, and the California Department of Alcoholic Beverage

Control. Mr. Sena received his bachelor of arts degree in criminal justice from California State University, San Bernardino.

I now recognize the gentleman from New Jersey, Ranking Member Payne, to introduce our next witness.

Mr. PAYNE. Thank you, Madam Chairwoman.

Paul Molitor serves as the assistant vice president of smart grid and special projects for the National Electrical Manufacturers Association. For 450 member companies of NEMA, he is responsible for monitoring the National smart grid effort and interfacing with electrical utilities, manufacturers, Federal agencies, and the U.S. Congress.

Paul was the first plenary secretary of the NIST Smart Grid Interoperability Panel, is active in the SGIP cybersecurity and internet protocol working groups and the International Electronical Commission Strategy Group 3 on the smart grid.

Welcome, sir.

Say that fast three times.

Mrs. BROOKS. The witnesses' full written statements—I want to thank you all for your written statements—they will appear in the record. Just as a reminder with the lighting system, you each will have 5 minutes and when you get to 1 minute you will see the yellow light and then the red light when your time is up.

So I will now recognize Ms. Stempfley for her 5 minutes.

STATEMENT OF ROBERTA STEMPFLEY, ACTING ASSISTANT SECRETARY, OFFICE OF CYBERSECURITY AND COMMUNICATIONS, NATIONAL PROTECTION AND PROGRAMS DIRECTORATE, U.S. DEPARTMENT OF HOMELAND SECURITY

Ms. STEMPFLEY. Thank you very much, Chairwoman Brooks, Chairman Meehan, Ranking Members Payne and Clarke, and distinguished Members of the committee. It certainly is a privilege to appear before you today to discuss the Department of Homeland Security's coordination with State, local, Tribal, and territorial emergency managers on cybersecurity issues.

As the Chairwoman pointed out, it is National Cybersecurity Awareness Month. In fact, it is the 10th anniversary of the beginning of National Cybersecurity Awareness Month. This week is an important week for us because we also transition in November to National Critical Infrastructure Security and Resilience Month, further demonstrating the alliance—the integration and necessary responsibility for looking at cyber and physical issues in a cohesive and coherent manner.

This month of October is the month where we get to further engage in public and private-sector stakeholder conversations about how to create safe, secure, and resilient cyber environment. Everyone has a role to play in cybersecurity and I am pleased to discuss the Department's efforts to engage State and local emergency managers as they build cybersecurity resilience into the networks and systems which they depend on in a daily basis.

America's cybersecurity is inextricably linked to our National economic viability. IT systems are interdependent, interconnected, and critical to our daily lives, from communications, travel, powering our homes, running our economy, and obtaining Government services.

DHS serves as the lead civilian Department responsible for co-ordinating National protection, prevention, mitigation, and recovery from cyber incidents, and we work regularly with business owners and operators to take steps to strengthen facilities and communities including the Nation's physical and cyber infrastructure. We are also committed to ensuring cyber space is supported by a secure and resilient infrastructure, enabling open communications, innovation, and prosperity while protecting privacy, confidentiality, and civil rights and civil liberties by design.

Protecting this infrastructure against growing and evolving cyber threats requires a layered approach. The Government's role in this effort is to share information and encourage enhanced security and resilience while identifying and addressing gaps not filled by the marketplace.

Providing effective cybersecurity services requires fostering relationships with those who own and operate communications infrastructure, members in the emergency responder community, and Federal, State, local, Tribal, and territorial partners. Indeed, as many of the communication technologies currently used by public safety and emergency services organizations are moving to internet-based—protocol-based environments there is an increasing awareness of the cyber limitations and vulnerabilities that our emergency service providers will face in conduct of their mission. It is important, therefore, for the Department to engage not just with chief information officers or chief information security officers at the State and local level, but also the emergency management and other officials for whom a cyber environment is equally important to accomplishing their mission.

The Department has initiated several activities focusing on ensuring State, local, Tribal, and territorial emergency managers are able to build cybersecurity resilience into those information and technology networks and systems upon which they depend.

Several of these efforts include production and delivery of a cyber infrastructure risk assessment for both the Nation-wide Public Safety Broadband Network and the emergency services sector; local pilot projects with emergency managers and critical infrastructure partners to better understand interconnections between those cyber and physical infrastructures and potential risks presented to the Nation; updating the National Emergency Communications Plan in coordination with the public safety community, which will discuss how cybersecurity has become a key consideration for public safety officials in these new IP-enabled technologies as that is more readily integrated into their operations; and the deployment of regionally-based advisors to promote cybersecurity awareness, program and policy coordination, information sharing, and risk analysis to their partners.

These cybersecurity advisors directly engage with State and local emergency centers; and partnerships with non-Federal public-sector stakeholders to protect critical network—for example, the Multi-State Information-Sharing and Analysis Center, which opened its Cybersecurity Operations Center in November 2010 and has enhanced the Department's situational awareness at the State and local level and allows the Department to provide cyber risk, vulnerability, and mitigation data quickly to State and local governments.

Specifically, since 2009 the National Cybersecurity and Communications Integration Center has responded to nearly half a million incident reports and has released more than 26,000 actionable cybersecurity alerts to public and private-sector partners. Of that, 7,270 were released in fiscal year 2013 alone. That is more than 20 a day.

DHS's servicing capabilities are designed to support emergency managers at all levels of engagement across education, planning, cyber incident response, and recovery activities. They are integral parts of reducing risk and building capabilities of our partners. As necessary, these relationships have to be leveraged in operational response efforts in order to meet those immediate and critical needs.

I thank you for the opportunity to testify with you today and I look forward to answering your questions.

[The prepared statement of Ms. Stempfley follows:]

PREPARED STATEMENT OF ROBERTA STEMPFLEY

OCTOBER 30, 2013

Chairwoman Brooks and Chairman Meehan, Ranking Members Payne and Clarke, and distinguished Members of the committee, it is a pleasure to appear before you today to discuss the Department of Homeland Security's (DHS) coordination with State, local, Tribal, and territorial (SLTT) emergency managers on cybersecurity issues. This October marks the 10th anniversary of National Cyber Security Awareness Month, which is an opportunity to further engage public and private-sector stakeholders to create a safe, secure, and resilient cyber environment. Everyone has a role to play in cybersecurity and I am pleased to discuss the Department's efforts to engage SLTT emergency managers as they build cybersecurity resilience into those networks and systems upon which they depend on a daily basis.

America's cybersecurity is inextricably linked to our Nation's economic vitality— IT systems are interdependent, interconnected, and critical to our daily lives—from communication, travel, and powering our homes, to running our economy, and obtaining Government services. DHS is the lead Federal civilian department responsible for coordinating the National protection, prevention, mitigation, and recovery from cyber incidents and works regularly with business owners and operators to take steps to strengthen their facilities and communities, which include the Nation's physical and cyber infrastructure. We are also committed to ensuring cyberspace is supported by a secure and resilient infrastructure that enables open communication, innovation, and prosperity while protecting privacy, confidentiality, and civil rights and civil liberties by design.

CYBERSECURITY SUPPORT TO SLTT EMERGENCY MANAGERS

Protecting this infrastructure against growing and evolving cyber threats requires a layered approach. The Government's role in this effort is to share information and encourage enhanced security and resilience, while identifying and addressing gaps not filled by the marketplace. Providing effective cybersecurity services requires fostering relationships with those who own and operate the communications infrastructure, members of the emergency responder community, and Federal, State, local, Tribal, and territorial partners. Indeed, as many of the communications technologies currently used by public safety and emergency services organizations move to an Internet Protocol (IP)-based environment, there is an increase in the cyber vulnerabilities of our emergency services providers in the conduct of their mission. It is important, therefore, for the Department to engage not just Chief Information Officers (CIO) or Chief Information Security Officers (CISO) at the SLTT level, but also the emergency managers and other officials for whom a secure cyber environment is equally as important to accomplishing their mission.

The Department has initiated several activities focused on ensuring SLTT emergency managers are able to build cybersecurity resilience into those information and technology networks and systems upon which they depend. Cyber dependencies and interdependencies require interactions between several different DHS organizations and SLTT partners in order to address this complex need. DHS has been forward-thinking as the reliance upon cyber systems has grown and our engagements have been on-going.

PREVIOUS EFFORTS

- *Regionally-Based Cybersecurity Advisors.*—The Cybersecurity Advisors (CSA) program was created and implemented by CS&C in 2010. The regionally-deployed personnel promote cybersecurity awareness, program and policy coordination, information sharing, and risk analysis to their partners, including emergency managers. Over the last year, CSAs have had direct engagement with 13 State or local emergency centers. In addition, the Department has conducted Cyber Resilience Reviews and assessments and provided support to numerous National Security Special Events, including planning for events such as the Super Bowl, and the G8 with the City of Chicago's Office of Emergency Management & Communications.
- *Emergency Services Sector Cyber Risk Assessment.*—Encompassing a wide range of emergency response functions carried out by five disciplines,[1] in 2012 the Emergency Services Sector completed a Cyber Risk Assessment, which provides a risk profile to enhance the security and resilience of the Emergency Services Sector disciplines. It is an effort to establish a baseline of cyber risks across the sector, to ensure Federal resources are applied where they offer the most benefit for mitigating risk, and to encourage a similar risk-based allocation of resources within State and local entities and the private sector. Emergency managers from local, State, and Federal government actively participated in the development process to ensure the assessment provided practical guidance for the public safety community. The Department continues to meet with officials from stakeholder associations such as the National Emergency Management Association to discuss next steps, including developing a workforce training program for emergency managers in order to increase cybersecurity capabilities within the emergency management community.
- *Local Pilot Projects with Emergency Managers and Critical Infrastructure Partners.*—DHS is conducting three pilots to better understand the interconnections between cyber and physical infrastructure and the potential risks to the Nation. The first pilot, initiated in 2012, worked closely with Charlotte, NC emergency planners and neighboring communities to examine how a potential cyber attack could disrupt communications or other infrastructure operations. The work provided additional ways for planners to mitigate potential cyber impacts and, as a result of the pilot, commercial facilities adopted additional security practices to shore up potential weaknesses.

    The second pilot is underway with the State of New Jersey examining the interrelationship between IT, communications, and physical security. The pilot involves five water and wastewater facilities and has received praise from the State Office of Homeland Security and our water sector partners. As a result of initial findings, water facilities have taken immediate action to mitigate previously unknown vulnerabilities.

    The third pilot is a joint cyber-physical assessment of a Federal facility in Washington, DC to develop a common approach for identifying cybersecurity vulnerabilities affecting security systems of Federally-protected facilities, including electrical, HVAC, water, telecommunications, and security control systems.

    The lessons from these pilots have been incorporated into our integrated physical and cyber Regional Resiliency Assessment Program (RRAP). This is helping strengthen the partnership we already have; build new relationships between SLTT CIOs, first responders, and critical infrastructure owners and operators; and lay the foundation increased collaboration to increase cybersecurity resilience.
- *Nation-wide Public Safety Broadband Network (NPSBN) Cyber Infrastructure Risk Assessment.*—The development and deployment of an IP-based network for public safety will represent a leap forward in communications capabilities for first responders, law enforcement, and other users of the NPSBN. However, the move to such a network presents a challenge for the emergency management community to identify threats to and vulnerabilities of cyber infrastructure in the NPSBN that could affect the network's reliability and security. DHS is

[1] Law Enforcement; Fire and Emergency Services; Emergency Management; Emergency Medical Services; and Public Works.

working with the First Responder Network Authority (FirstNet) and the public safety community to identify cyber risks and develop potential responses to those risks. In 2013, OEC developed the NPSBN Cyber Infrastructure Risk Assessment to provide FirstNet with a how-to guide to address the top cyber risks that the network may face, and is now working with FirstNet to ensure a more resilient network design that will integrate security and resilience into the overall physical and cyber aspects of the NPSBN.

- *Cyber Threat Information Sharing.*—In June 2013, DHS established "sharelines" in compliance with Executive Order (EO) 13636 and Presidential Policy Directive (PPD)–21 to help increase the volume, timeliness, and quality of cyber threat information shared with U.S. private-sector entities, to include SLTT owners and operators, so that these entities may better protect and defend themselves against cyber threats. Sharelines "facilitate the creation and dissemination of unclassified cyber threat reports to targeted private-sector entities owned or operating within the United States, as well as Federal, State, local, Tribal, and territorial partners" in a timely manner.

ON-GOING EFFORTS

DHS continues to build upon the relationships we have established throughout the Emergency Services Sector through strategic and operational efforts to provide solutions to our SLTT partners. On-going efforts within DHS consist of:

- *Update to the National Emergency Communications Plan.*—DHS is updating the National Emergency Communications Plan (NECP) in coordination with the public safety community to enhance planning, preparation, and security of broadband technologies used during response operations. The Plan will discuss how cybersecurity has become a key consideration for public safety officials as new IP-enabled technology is increasingly integrated into operations. The NECP will endorse a multi-faceted approach to ensure the confidentiality, integrity, and availability of sensitive data. For example, comprehensive cyber training and education on the proper use and security of devices and applications, phishing, malware, other potential threats, and how to stay on guard against attacks will be recommended.
- *9–1–1 Centers: Next Generation 9–1–1 and Telephonic Denial of Service.*—Updated 9–1–1 infrastructure utilizes public voice, data, and video capabilities, which introduce new vulnerabilities into 9–1–1 systems. Separately, 9–1–1 centers have been targeted by telephonic denial of service (TDOS) attacks that overwhelm Public Safety Answering Points' administrative lines. These attacks inundate a 9–1–1 call center with a high volume of calls, overwhelming the system's ability to process calls and tying up the system from receiving legitimate calls. DHS, through the NCCIC, has worked on the development and dissemination of techniques for mitigating and managing these TDOS attacks in order to allow emergency management agencies to continue to provide these critical services to the public.
- *Protective Security Advisors (PSAs).*—Within the Office of Infrastructure Protection, PSAs serve as the nexus of our infrastructure security and coordination efforts at the Federal, State, local, Tribal, and territorial levels and serve as DHS's on-site critical infrastructure and vulnerability assessment specialists. PSAs have also been working with CS&C to better coordinate assessments and as a result approximately half of cybersecurity site assessments administered by CS&C were conducted in tandem with PSAs—an example of how we are working to better and more effectively integrate our physical and cybersecurity efforts across NPPD and the Department.
- *Multi-State Information Sharing and Analysis Center (MS–ISAC).*—DHS builds partnerships with non-Federal public-sector stakeholders to protect critical network systems. For example, the Multi-State Information Sharing and Analysis Center (MS–ISAC) opened its Cyber Security Operations Center in November 2010, which has enhanced the National Cybersecurity & Communications Integration Center (NCCIC) situational awareness at the State and local government level and allows the Federal Government to quickly and efficiently provide critical cyber risk, vulnerability, and mitigation data to State and local governments. Since 2009, the NCCIC has responded to nearly a half a million incident reports and released more than 26,000 actionable cybersecurity alerts to our public and private-sector partners.

Membership in the MS–ISAC consists of State and local CISOs and other leadership from all 50 State governments, the District of Columbia, 373 local governments, three territories, five Tribes, and 24 educational institutions. It provides valuable information and lessons learned on cyber threats, exploitations, vulnerabilities, consequences, incidents, and direct assistance with responding to and recovering from cyber attacks and compromises. The MS–ISAC runs a 24-hour watch and warning security operations center that provides real-time network monitoring, dissemination of early cyber threat warnings, vulnerability identification and mitigation, along with education and outreach aimed to reduce risk to the Nation's SLTT government cyber domain. This year the MS–ISAC developed a plan to increase engagement with emergency managers and fusion centers.

OPERATIONAL EFFORTS

Assuring the security and reliability of critical information networks is vital across all critical infrastructure sectors, including the Emergency Services Sector, which is charged with saving lives, protecting property and the environment, assisting communities impacted by disasters, and aiding recovery from emergencies. DHS is uniquely positioned to improve the cybersecurity posture of our stakeholders.

NATIONAL PROTECTION AND PROGRAMS DIRECTORATE

The Offices of the National Protection Programs Directorate interact daily with State and local officials and emergency managers on communications and cybersecurity issues to strengthen infrastructure, educate citizens, and respond to and recover from on-line threats and attacks.
- *Cybersecurity and Communications.*—CS&C maintains an overall focus on reducing risk to the communications and information technology infrastructures and the sectors that depend upon them, as well as providing threat and vulnerability information and enabling timely response and recovery of these infrastructures under all circumstances. We execute our mission by supporting 24×7 information sharing, analysis, and incident response through the National Cybersecurity Communications Integration Center (NCCIC); facilitating interoperable emergency communications through our Office of Emergency Communications (OEC); advancing technology solutions for private and public-sector partners; providing tools and capabilities to ensure the security of Federal civilian Executive branch networks; and engaging in strategic level coordination for the Department with stakeholders on cybersecurity and communications issues. Additionally OEC has strong ties to emergency managers through its outreach to State-Wide Interoperability Coordinators (SWIC) who State officials who are the primary points of contact for communications interoperability issues. These produce State-Wide Interoperability Plans which establish governance, processes, and procedures to support first-responder communication. These strong relationships also help SLTT leverage other resources such as fusion centers.
- *Office of Infrastructure Protection.*—The Office of Infrastructure Protection within NPPD leads and coordinates National programs and policies on critical infrastructure, including through implementation of the National Infrastructure Protection Plan (NIPP). The NIPP establishes the framework for integrating the Nation's various critical infrastructure protection and resilience initiatives into a coordinated effort, and provides the structure through which DHS, in partnership with Government and industry, implements programs and activities to protect critical infrastructure, promote National preparedness, and enhance incident response. As the NIPP is updated based on the requirements of Presidential Policy Directive 21, Critical Infrastructure Security and Resilience, NPPD will work with critical infrastructure stakeholders to focus the revision on enhanced integration of cyber and physical risk management, requirements for increased resilience, and recognition for the need for enhanced information-sharing and situational awareness. As we work to update the NIPP we will support the Emergency Services Sector to ensure that we inform first responders in their preparation for cyber incidents.

COORDINATED CYBER/PHYSICAL RESPONSE

While the National Cybersecurity Communications Integration Center (NCCIC) processes incident reports, issues actionable cybersecurity alerts, and deploys on-site incident response fly-away teams to critical infrastructure organizations to assist with analysis and recovery efforts of a cyber incident, the National Infrastructure Coordinating Center (NICC) provides situational awareness of threats to physical critical infrastructure, incident response support, and business reconstitution assistance. In addition to this coordination, as incidents or threats occur, PSAs living in communities across the country provide the Department with a 24/7 capability to assist in developing a common operational picture for critical infrastructure. NPPD efforts to integrate physical and cybersecurity have provided benefits during incidents including:

- *Hurricane Sandy.*—NPPD operational efforts were able to facilitate much-needed fuel deliveries to critical telecommunication sites in lower Manhattan in order to fuel generators and keep the facilities operational in recent events like Hurricane Sandy. After PSAs were notified of the fuel supply shortage, NPPD provided analysis on the wide-spread impact if the telecommunications facility lost power, while the NCCIC worked with its public and private-sector partners to identify a fuel supply and coordinate its delivery to the critical site.
- *Boston Marathon Bombing.*—OEC worked closely with public safety agencies in the Metro Boston Homeland Security Region and with the Commonwealth of Massachusetts on several key emergency communications initiatives prior to the 2013 marathon including observing public safety communications during previous marathons and events and offering suggestions to help strengthen the region's capabilities and improve coordination. Three years later, DHS saw many of the recommendations from this assessment in action in response to the bombings, including the region's use of a detailed communications plan (ICS Form 205) for the event that assigned radio channels to various agencies and functions.

CONCLUSION

DHS provides a variety of services and capabilities designed to support emergency managers at all levels of engagement, across education, planning, cyber-incident response, and recovery activities. The services and capabilities are all integral parts of reducing risk and building capacity of our SLTT partners. As necessary, those relationships are leveraged in operational response efforts in order to meet immediate, critical needs. As technologies continue to advance and the dependencies and interdependencies between the sectors and systems continue to advance along with them, DHS will continue to work with emergency managers in a holistic fashion to plan, prepare, mitigate, and build resilience into those information and technology networks and systems upon which they depend on a daily basis. Thank you for this opportunity to testify, and I look forward to answering any questions you may have.

Mrs. BROOKS. Thank you, Ms. Stempfley.

The Chairwoman now recognizes Mr. English for 5 minutes.

STATEMENT OF CHARLEY ENGLISH, DIRECTOR, GEORGIA EMERGENCY MANAGEMENT AGENCY, TESTIFYING ON BEHALF OF NATIONAL EMERGENCY MANAGEMENT ASSOCIATION

Mr. ENGLISH. Thank you, Chairman Brooks, Chairman Meehan, and Ranking Members Payne and Clarke, for your foresight in having this hearing on bridging the gap between emergency management and the cybersecurity profession.

You know, in my profession we all have come to believe that the cyber threat is a very real threat but what we disagree on sometimes is what the extent of the consequences of that particular threat could be, whether or not it is just a matter of espionage or hackers trying to steal intellectual property or nation-states trying to uncover some type of technology that we have, or whether it is more of a theft of credit card and bank accounts and things of that nature, or whether or not, as Mr. Payne mentioned, the 9–1–1 system might be compromised in the middle of an event.

So we still have a differing opinion on that but the one thing that we don't have a difference of opinion on, and that is we can never again underestimate the creativity of those who want to harm us. Because if there is that will they will find a way, whether it is the lone hacker behind the computer screen, whether it is a group of terrorists that want to compromise one of our water treatment plants or dams, or if it is a nation-state trying to threaten us, we know that it would be a big mistake to underestimate that creativity and to underestimate the organizational skills of our enemies.

Of course in emergency management we are all about the business of warnings and managing the consequences of an event. As I was thinking about our friends in the cybersecurity business I thought, you know, it would be great if we could develop a relationship that exists between the CIOs in the State and emergency managers and across the country that is similar to that of the meteorologists. You know, that relationship is on autopilot. They are monitoring the weather. The conversation exists on a daily basis.

I thought about, well, you know, we have forged a new relationship in this country in the past 12 or 14 years with the law enforcement and the intel community and the emergency management profession. Early on that was a tough relationship to forge because of the security clearances and the lack of reciprocity and the whole information sharing and we were putting together a clash of cultures, if you will, because the emergency manager wants every agency and every person available to help alleviate the pain and suffering after an event and to help keep people out of harm's way. Naturally there are secrets that need to be kept, and so sometimes there was a little clash of cultures.

But we have made tremendous progress in the past 12 or 13 years in that regard and I think the same is true with the cybersecurity professionals and the emergency management community. This is a relationship that will mature and it is not a matter of that no one really wanted to—or didn't want to work together. I think everybody wanted to work together; we just weren't sure how we were supposed to work together.

So I think the challenge moving forward is not necessarily to create a new agency or start a new grant program, but maybe it is on us to teach one another about our professions and foster that relationship for the betterment of our country.

With that, I will yield the rest of my time. Thank you.

[The prepared statement of Mr. English follows:]

PREPARED STATEMENT OF CHARLEY ENGLISH

OCTOBER 30, 2013

INTRODUCTION

Chairman Brooks, Chairman Meehan, Ranking Members Payne and Clarke, and distinguished members of this panel—thank you for holding this hearing today on one of the most critical issues currently facing our Nation. Cybersecurity and the resultant vulnerabilities and consequences could easily match the impact of any significant natural disaster, so we must analyze these threats carefully and plan to manage them accordingly.

The establishment of this committee came about more than a decade ago in the wake of an attack which came from an under-appreciated threat. This morning, we stand at the precipice of another such attack—one from a potentially nameless, faceless, and equally under-appreciated adversary. The threat of a cyber attack not only surrounds us, but also poses the additional threat of compromising the response and recovery efforts to the consequences of such an attack.

Last summer, the Chairman of the House Intelligence Committee said he expects what he called "a catastrophic cyber attack in the next 12 to 24 months."

Earlier this year, former Secretary Napolitano said an incident on the scale of September 11 could happen "imminently."

The Defense Science Board went even further saying "coming cyber attacks could present an existential threat to the country."

As emergency managers, we operate in a world of consequence management. Accordingly, we must understand threats, protect vulnerabilities, and know how to manage consequences. As we examine the cyber threats facing this Nation, we cannot fall into a September 10, 2001, mindset. Our actions must be pro-active and consider all potential outcomes. We must never say, "it cannot happen here" nor shall we fear being labeled an "alarmist" by merely acknowledging the potential devastating consequences of this already validated threat.

THE THREAT

Plenty of experts remain ready and willing to provide thoughts and hypotheses regarding the current cybersecurity threat. The vulnerabilities and resulting consequences we face in these threats represent the "bottom-line" for the emergency management community. Vulnerabilities are points of attack and weaknesses to be exploited. The emergency management community must address the consequences of vulnerabilities being exploited, not just the existence of vulnerabilities themselves. In his report to Congress of March 12, 2013, Director of National Intelligence James Clapper outlined how "we are in a major transformation because our critical infrastructures, economy, personal lives, and even basic understanding of—and interaction with—the world are becoming more intertwined with digital technologies and the internet."

Such analyses are especially concerning as we continue witnessing a metamorphosis of the cyber threat. Once a means by which to conduct espionage and steal information, the realm of cybersecurity must now include an analysis on the security and viability of our critical infrastructure. At the RSA Cybersecurity Conference on March 1, 2012, former FBI Director Robert Mueller stated "to date, terrorists have not used the internet to launch a full-scale cyber attack. But we cannot underestimate their intent. In one hacker recruiting video, a terrorist proclaims that cyber warfare will be the warfare of the future." Only through good fortune have organized terrorist groups not yet taken a greater interest in cyber attacks. But such a day is certainly coming.

Earlier this year, Anonymous petitioned the White House to recognize hacking attacks as a legitimate form of protest. Their solicitation argued hacking is no different than marching in an Occupy Wall Street protect. We must consider how such an approach can be combatted through our current systems and processes. Even though some experts believe Anonymous represents no true threat, others believe such an organization could bring down part of the U.S. electric power grid. Most recently, the homeland security community has been concerned with and has devoted significant resources to combatting Homegrown Violent Extremists (HVE). It is reasonable to conclude that these individuals, acting alone or in small groups, certainly have the motivation and expertise to conduct a cyber attack.

Unfortunately, cyber threats represent risks far more diverse than most any other we face. While nation-states like Iran present a significant cyber threat, the greatest cyber threat from a nation likely comes from China where hacking stands as an official policy. Just recently, the Chief of Staff of the People's Liberation Army put the cyber threat into perspective when he suggested such an attack could be as serious as a nuclear bomb. Even though in his report to Congress Director Clapper said "advanced cyber actors—such as Russia and China—are unlikely to launch such a devastating attack against the United States outside of a military conflict or crisis that they believe threatens their vital interest," the threat alone should be enough to garner the attention of the homeland security and emergency management community.

ADDRESSING VULNERABILITIES & CONSEQUENCES

Emergency managers stand increasingly concerned regarding the inter-connectedness of the threat and everyday life in America. Citizens can evacuate in anticipation of a hurricane. Strong building codes and safe rooms can protect lives in anticipation of earthquakes or tornadoes. But as we consider the breadth and depth of our reliance on the cyber infrastructure, the emergency response efforts regarding consequence management could easily overwhelm local, State, and Federal assets due to the interdependencies of critical infrastructure and key resource protection as well as the ease of vulnerability exploitation from a cyber attack. Consider this short list of potential hazards and vulnerabilities:

- Computer-controlled dams protecting a low-lying community,
- National power grids and nuclear power plants,
- Emergency Alert Systems (EAS) and 9–1–1 systems,
- Traffic systems utilized to evacuate a population,

- Banking systems ranging from Wall Street to basic on-line transfers and ATM withdrawals,
- The National airline and air traffic control network,
- Complex and simple communications systems from Emergency Operations Centers to the basic smartphone, and
- Water supply networks and waste management systems.

Even many of today's commonly-used Global Positioning System (GPS), which relies heavily on a cyber structure, represents a potential target vulnerable to attack. Taken by themselves, each of these threats could have devastating effects. But emergency managers must consider a potential event impacting any number of combinations of these systems.

The connectivity of systems today makes the consequences of a cyber attack more significant at all levels of government and throughout the private sector. Admittedly, emergency managers often defer cybersecurity issues to information technology (IT) officials; yet State IT professionals and other leaders will rely on emergency managers to respond to the consequences of an attack. The emergency management and IT communities must establish relationships and engage in coordinated planning and information sharing long before an event occurs.

States such as Michigan continue taking a keen interest in how to manage the cybersecurity threat. Through robust coordination and planning at the State level, Michigan approaches cybersecurity with the same concepts as those employed when preparing for and responding to natural or terrorist threats.

The Michigan Cyber Initiative brings together many State agencies including the Michigan National Guard, State Police, and Department of Technology, Management, and Budget in a coordinated effort to enhance detection of cyber attacks and integrate response systems. The Michigan Cyber Initiative integrates the Michigan Cyber Command Center, Michigan Cyber Defense Response Team, and Michigan Intelligence Operations Center to enhance prevention, early detection and rapid response, and control, management, and restoration. The Michigan Online Cyber Toolkit raises awareness and preparedness for all the components of the cyber ecosystem. The toolkit provides best practices and easy steps for safeguarding a vulnerable environment. It also offers the chance for users to quiz themselves, download posters and calendars, and obtain tip sheets on how to solve on-line problems. The toolkit is broken down by sectors including homes, businesses, Government, and schools.

Michigan is clearly working hand-in-hand with various components in ensuring the addressing of cybersecurity across all disciplines. Even as these relationships continue developing in other States, however, we must examine how the consequences of a cyber attack will be addressed. Furthermore, we must complete an honest assessment of necessary authorities and whether they represent adequate resources to respond to such an attack.

CURRENT AUTHORITIES

As NEMA received briefings on the Quadrennial Homeland Security Review (QHSR) of the Department of Homeland Security (DHS), we inquired as to whether the Department would examine physical impacts of cybersecurity. They informed us that while the QHSR would include some examination of the consequences of a cyber attack, the Department's analysis of past cyber attacks reveal very few physical impacts constituting a significant threat to safety and life. We want to ensure that all potential consequences of a cyber attack are thoroughly considered. We feel like anything less is short-sighted and underestimates the ability and creativity of the enemy whether the enemy is foreign or domestic. Our country has on several occasions witnessed the creativity of those who are intent on harming us. There have been shoes, printer cartridges, underwear, and pressure cookers used as bombs and, of course, airplanes used as missiles.

But even States struggle in addressing this threat. In a survey completed in February of this year, NEMA learned:

- 79.1 percent of States interpret the consequences of a cyber attack under statutes as "All Hazards" versus 20.9 percent which list it as a specific hazard.
- 62.8 percent of States do not maintain a law enforcement-specific component to any of the State statutes relating to cyber-response.
- No clear best practice exists in assigning responsibility of coordination of resources to prepare for, respond to, or recover from a cyber attack with only 41.9 percent of States citing such a directive. Of the 41.9 percent responsibility ranges from the emergency management to IT, homeland security, and the fusion center.

With States remaining somewhat unclear on the appropriate course of action, the current lack of a cohesive National strategy at the Federal level is not surprising. We hope that the response strategy matures the Federal Government will not over-bureaucratize the process and bury State and local governments in a sea of reports, guidance documents, and processes.

We think it is prudent to continue the insistence of metrics and return on investment calculations on the millions of dollars in initiatives funded at DHS. Some organizations, however, such as the Office of Cybersecurity and Communication (CS&C) within DHS continue admirable work in their outreach to State and local officials. The effort must be comprehensive and coordinated in order to ensure all the nuances of the threat receive appropriate attention. Federal efforts must be structured in concert with States and locals rather than adopting a top-down approach.

But underlying statutory authorities are equally unclear. During the NEMA Annual Emergency Management Policy & Leadership Forum in Seattle, Washington last year, a panel of experts addressed the statutory issue. According to the panelists including a former Adjutant General, a DHS Deputy Assistant Secretary, and several State Homeland Security Advisors, the Civil Defense Act of 1950 (81–950) represents the only law potentially applicable to a potential cyber attack. Since the original intent of this Act provided for the response to a nuclear attack from the Soviet Union, the time to explore the efficacy of our current statutory authorities is now. Current statutory authorities are lacking regarding cyber attacks and are currently under revision; however, the recent remark by President Obama that a cyber attack can now be classified as an "act of war" significantly changes the "environment." This recent change should be taken into consideration when speaking of statutory authorities and can be used to further illustrate the fluid and uncertain nature of the issue.

Most emergency managers will turn to the Robert T. Stafford Disaster Relief and Emergency Assistance Act (Pub. L. 92–288). Unless the consequences of a cyber attack truly have catastrophic and physical consequences, however, the Stafford Act will be limited. Unfortunately, too many of the legislative fixes currently under consideration in Congress only address the prevention and preparedness side of cybersecurity. While the pre-event aspects of cybersecurity maintain a high level of importance, so too will the post-event considerations.

MOVING FORWARD

The purpose of this hearing is to ensure consequence management resulting from a cyber attack is recognized as a priority with emphasis equal to preparedness measures. As Congress considers legislative options, the needs of the State and locals ultimately responsible for the consequences of a cyber attack must be first and foremost. In May of last year, NEMA joined with the American Public Works Association, Council of State Governments, International City/County Management Association, National Association of Counties, National Association of State Chief Information Officers, National Association of Telecommunications Officers and Advisors, National Conference of State Legislatures, the National League of Cities, and the International Association of Emergency Managers to ask Congress for your consideration of key principles and values when considering cybersecurity legislation. The outlined principles and values include:

1. State and local governments must be viewed as critical stakeholders in National cybersecurity efforts.—Both execute programs overseen and funded by Federal agencies, and frequently are custodians of Federal data. They also operate and manage critical infrastructure including data centers and networks which are necessary for basic homeland security and emergency management functions. Therefore, the Federal Government must work with State and local government to share threat information and to provide technical support to protect computer networks and other related critical infrastructure.

2. The Federal Government must avoid unfunded mandates on State and local partners.—Public budgets are still strained at all levels of government, and while State and local stakeholders wish to contribute to the overall cybersecurity effort, the ability to independently fund initiatives at this time is unlikely. Likewise, Federal program requirements and directives have traditionally hindered State and local governments from potentially achieving economies of scale.

3. Federal, State, and local governments should collaborate to invest in cybersecurity awareness, education, and training for public-sector employees, contractors, and private citizens.

4. The civil liberties and privacy of all citizens must be maintained while also establishing the safety and stability of the internet and electronic communica-

tions.—This is especially critical as governments continue to expand on-line and electronic services. Safeguarding public-sector data that includes personal information of citizens will require cooperation and collaboration on data standards and cybersecurity methodology at all levels of government.

5. Many Federal initiatives fund internet and information security programs.— However, without cross-cutting communication and coordinated assets, the efforts will not realize maximum efficiency and impact. If there are privacy and security requirements that are pre-conditions of Federal programs and funding they must be uniformly interpreted and implemented across all agencies and levels.

Earlier this year, NEMA attempted an effort to address cybersecurity consequences simply from the emergency management standpoint. A workgroup comprised of many NEMA members has worked since March in developing a doctrine for emergency management directors to consider. Unfortunately, even this effort proved more difficult than originally anticipated, and instead of continuing alone, NEMA has since joined forces with the National Governors Association (NGA) in their cybersecurity efforts.

NGA recently released a "Call to Action for Governors for Cybersecurity." The document outlines guiding principles, immediate actions to protect States, provides multiple examples from various States, and discusses a path forward. The guiding principles include supporting Governors, remaining actionable, reducing complexity, protecting privacy, employing technologically-neutral solutions, promoting flexible federalism, generating metrics, and promoting the use of incentives. NEMA looks forward to continuing our work with NGA as this complex issue gains increased attention.

The combined capacity of Federal, State, and local governments to adequately safeguard the Nation's critical infrastructure systems remains essential to ensuring effective operations across the full spectrum of the threats we face. Furthermore, in order for communities to effectively manage emergency situations, cyber systems must be resilient to acts of terrorism, attacks, and natural disasters.

CONCLUSION

Cybersecurity represents the most complex threat and advanced vulnerabilities we as a Nation face. We must ensure consequence management resulting from a cyber attack is recognized as a priority with emphasis equal to preparedness measures. The challenge for all of us will be to examine it through a new prism, for we will fail if we respond the same way as always. This is not a traditional threat and reaches across sectors of our society which may have never before worked together. Cyber threats can only be addressed through collaboration, planning, and a deep understanding of the potential consequences. For if we fail either through prevention or response, the impacts truly could be disastrous.

Thank you.

Mrs. BROOKS. Thank you, Mr. English.

The Chairwoman now recognizes Dr. Orgeron for 5 minutes.

STATEMENT OF CRAIG ORGERON, CIO AND EXECUTIVE DIRECTOR, DEPARTMENT OF INFORMATION TECHNOLOGY SERVICES, STATE OF MISSISSIPPI, TESTIFYING ON BEHALF OF NATIONAL ASSOCIATION OF STATE CHIEF INFORMATION OFFICERS

Mr. ORGERON. Thank you Chairs Brooks and Meehan, Ranking Members Payne and Clarke, and Members of the committee, for inviting me to speak today. I am truly honored by the invitation.

As the executive director of the Mississippi Department of ITS, Information Technology Services, as well as president of the National Association of State Chief Information Officers, better known as NASCIO, I can report that each year States are facing greater numbers of evolving and sophisticated cyber threats. The State of Mississippi's IT systems, like systems from all States, face cyber attacks ranging from a few thousand attempts to as many as 10 million a day—some domestic, many international. To win this on-going battle, State IT experts have to be right every time while hackers need to be only right once.

As these attacks continue to grow more sophisticated, both public and private-sector entities will need to develop better tools and increase collaboration to both deter attacks and plan a coordinated response to contain the damage from successful attacks. This ultimately requires a multi-sector approach with all levels of Government and private industry working together.

State CIOs are, indeed, at the table in securing State systems. Each year NASCIO surveys its membership. Our 2013 survey, which I have attached to my written testimony, shows how State CIOs are taking important steps toward building a more secure State IT environment. However, there are still known gaps.

According to our survey data, the State CIO role in disaster recovery appears to be increasing yearly. State CIOs generally coordinate with other State officials in restoring and maintaining infrastructure and communication services to help their State respond to and recover from natural and man-made disasters. When asked about their concerns, State CIOs put increasingly sophisticated threats to their systems followed closely by a lack of funding and inadequate availability of security professionals at the top of their list.

As the Federal Government and private sector ramp up their defenses against sophisticated hackers, State governments are becoming prime targets of foreign state-sponsored entities and international crime syndicates. These hackers can remain in State systems monitoring data and waiting to unleash significant harm. In worst-case scenarios, a sophisticated hack on public safety systems or critical infrastructure could coincide with a physical attack or a natural disaster to impede the ability of authorities to respond to one or both events.

It is well-known that when compared with the private sector and the Federal Government, States do not have comparable resources and tools to provide similar levels of protection to their systems despite the fact that they often maintain the same sensitive information and key critical infrastructure. This is only partly a financial issue; it is also a policy and a skilled personnel issue. On the latter two fronts, there is a great deal the Federal Government can do to help State governments improve preparedness and respond to cyber attacks.

I have included many of NASCIO's policy recommendations in my testimony but here are five areas: First, flexibility at the State level. Federal resources in support to States must respect and bolster the State organizations. Public-sector cybersecurity is in its infancy. Best practices must be shared but diverse approaches, particularly when it comes to governance, information sharing, and methodology, should be nurtured.

Second, increasing the workforce: Expanding Federal scholarships to study cybersecurity in exchange for working several years in the Federal Government or for State or local governments has a two-fold benefit of both better protecting our citizens and expanding available talent pools of cybersecurity experts.

Third, modernizing Federal regulations: Congress should consider working with NASCIO and the States to update the Federal

Information Security Management Act, or FISMA, with cybersecurity rules that better conform to universal, outcome-based standards that would provide both Federal agencies and States with better security as well as greater efficiencies.

Updating homeland security funding: Efforts to utilize existing Federal programs to better State governments in protecting the Nation against cyber attacks should also be explored. More than 10 years out from September 11, 2001, homeland security grants should be reformed to reflect the current threats faced by our States and localities.

Last, applying what we know: NASCIO believes the National Cybersecurity Review, or NCSR, is an excellent opportunity to review our National preparedness and provide resources and technical assistance to fill the gaps in our defenses. Holding hearings such as this one and finding ways to share information and resources will be crucial moving forward.

We ask that Congress continue to work with the States in identifying ways to protect our Nation's digital assets.

Thank you for the opportunity to testify and your time today.

[The prepared statement of Mr. Orgeron follows:]

PREPARED STATEMENT OF CRAIG ORGERON

OCTOBER 30, 2013

Thank you Chairs Brooks and Meehan, Ranking Members Payne and Clarke, and Members of the committee, for inviting me to speak to you today. I am honored by the invitation. As we wrap up Cybersecurity Awareness Month it is timely that we are having this hearing on one of our Nation's most significant vulnerabilities.

As executive director of the Mississippi Department of Information Technology Services (ITS), as well as president of the National Association of State Chief Information Officers, better known as NASCIO, I can report that each year States are facing greater numbers of evolving and sophisticated cyber attacks. In addition to States serving as a repository of sensitive data about our citizens and homeland, States increasingly utilize the on-line environment to deliver vital services, maintain critical infrastructure such as public utilities, and ensure our first responders receive the data they need in crisis situations. State government IT systems are a vital component of the Nation's critical infrastructure.

Today, with this testimony, I want to provide the committee information on the readiness of our State governments to defend against and respond to major cyber attacks, as well as opportunities to collaborate to minimize the risk to our Nation. I hope to give you a sense of the threat landscape and how States and the Federal Government, along with the private sector, can work together to better secure our homeland.

State governments are at risk from a host of new and aggressive security threats that require a formal strategy, adequate resources, and constant vigilance. Cybersecurity continues to be one of the major "hot button" issues for State CIOs and one that receives increasing attention from Governors and other elected officials.

State CIOs are taking the lead in securing State systems. According to NASCIO's 2013 survey of State CIOs conducted by in collaboration with TechAmerica and Grant Thornton LLP, significant improvements have been made in the last few years. Over three-quarters of States have adopted a cybersecurity framework, implemented continuous vulnerability monitoring capabilities, and developed security awareness training for employees and third-party contractors. These are key steps toward building a more secure State cyber environment. Unfortunately, less than half of States are documenting the effectiveness of the cybersecurity program they have in place, and even fewer have developed a cybersecurity disruption response plan.

In the same survey, CIOs were asked about the major barriers they faced in addressing cybersecurity. The increasing sophistication of threats, followed closely by a lack of funding and inadequate availability of security professionals, topped the list. Additionally, the survey data reveals that only 8 percent of States have implemented identity and access management of State data systems across the enterprise, although 42 percent of respondents noted an in-process implementation.

The State CIO role in disaster recovery appears to be increasing each year. According to the NASCIO 2013 survey almost two-thirds of States pursue a federated strategy to disaster recovery, with responsibilities split between the CIO and State departments and agencies. The survey also queried State CIOs regarding their role in helping their State respond to and recover from a natural or man-made disaster. The survey results show almost all CIOs see their role as one of coordinating with other State officials and restoring and maintaining infrastructure and communications services. I have attached the full results of this survey to my testimony today, along with the 2012 Deloitte-NASCIO Cybersecurity Study entitled "State governments at Risk," for your further review.*

The State of Mississippi's IT systems, like systems from all States, face cyber attacks every day, ranging from a few thousand attempts to as many as 10 million per day—some domestic, many international. To win this on-going battle, State IT experts have to be right every time, while hackers need to only be right once. As these attacks continue to grow more sophisticated, both public and private-sector entities will need to develop better tools and increase collaboration to both deter attacks and plan a coordinated response to contain the damage from successful attacks. This ultimately requires a multi-sector approach, with all levels of government and private industry working together. Securing systems in cyberspace, and responding to successful hacking attempts, has little in common with traditional emergency management after a disaster. Advanced cyber threats are much more akin to an aggressive, new strain of virus: The threat is diffuse, and almost impossible to prevent before it comes into being. In addition, just like a new viral strain, it takes time to properly identify and contain the virus, educate the populous about how to avoid contracting it, and treat those infected.

As the Federal Government and private sector ramp up their defenses against sophisticated hackers, State governments are becoming a prime target of foreign, state-sponsored entities, and international crime syndicates. Sophisticated hackers may hide in IT systems for years—creating what is referred to as an "advanced persistent threat." These hackers can remain in State systems monitoring data and waiting to unleash significant harm to our Nation's financial systems, transportation systems, supply chain, and key utilities such as the electrical grid, and pipelines, to name a few. In worst-case scenarios, a sophisticated hack on public safety communication systems or critical infrastructure could coincide with a physical attack or natural disaster to impede the ability of authorities to respond to one or both events.

Elected leaders at all levels have come to understand that cybersecurity is a significant issue that requires their attention. The National Governors Association (NGA) is working with the National Emergency Management Association (NEMA), NASCIO, and members of the private sector, to build upon this greater understanding. Based on this collaboration, NGA released "A Call to Action for Governors for Cybersecurity," which provides strategic recommendations Governors can immediately adopt to improve their State's cybersecurity posture. By gaining support from the Governor's office, a State can tackle key issues of governance and create an authority structure that builds comprehensive cybersecurity across the State enterprise. It is well-known that when compared with the private sector and the Federal Government, States do not have comparable resources and tools to provide similar levels of protection to their systems, despite the fact that they often maintain the same sensitive information and key critical infrastructure.

This is only partially a financial issue—it is also a policy and skilled personnel issue. On the latter two fronts, there is a great deal the Federal Government can do to help State governments improve preparedness and response to cyber attacks.

On policy, perhaps the single key to ensuring a substantial attack does not blindside us is the Federal Government facilitating greater information sharing between Federal agencies, the private sector, and State and local partners. NASCIO believes the implementation of Executive Order 13636 and Presidential Policy Directive 21 will be a first step to achieving these goals.

As each State's cybersecurity level of maturity and governance is different, NASCIO would be concerned about any effort by the Federal Government to designate a single State entity as the responsible point for sharing and disseminating information between State and Federal entities. Such decisions should ultimately be left to each State's Governor to fit their model of cyber governance. Just as each State has different geography and vulnerabilities to extreme weather or man-made disasters, State Information Technology systems and the governance of those IT sys-

---

*The information has been retained in committee files.

tems are very different. Federal resources and support to States must respect and bolster the State organizations.

States rely on multiple external resources for threat information, such as the Multi-State Information Sharing and Analysis Center (MS–ISAC), United States Computer Emergency Readiness Team (US–CERT), and FBI's InfraGuard. States then act on this information through various channels: Some States have built a sophisticated cyber capacity at their State fusion center, others have bolstered the authority of their Office of Information Technology, and some coordinate with a cyber division of their State National Guard. The Federal Government should support all these approaches. Public sector cybersecurity is in its infancy; best practices must be shared, but diverse approaches—particularly when it comes to governance and methodology—should be nurtured.

Due to the diverse landscape at the State level, the Federal Government must be as inclusive as possible in disseminating threat information, and work outside the public safety and intelligence sector's traditional one-to-many comfort zone. Cybersecurity works best when more people have an understanding of the threats. Therefore, NASCIO and its members applaud the on-going effort to provide greater declassification of cyber threat information. We hope this will be followed by collaborative effort to standardize information exchange models for sharing threat data.

Classified threats will always exist, though, and therefore, greater access to classified information is needed at the top echelons of State government. As of now, the U.S. Department of Homeland Security (DHS) will only provide State governments with two Top Secret clearances. Typically, these go to the Governor and their homeland security advisor or director of public safety. This means in many States, chief information officers or their chief information security officers are not cleared to the appropriate level to receive vital information from the intelligence community on the most advanced international threats against our networks. This should be remedied.

Additionally, while opportunities for limited Federal assistance for cyber threats have been included in the National Preparedness Grant Program (NPGP), the formulaic structure of the program means States do not have enough funding to do much more than maintain legacy homeland security investments and administer grants to local governments. For NPGP to meet the current threats faced by our States and localities, changes will need to be made by Congress and the administration.

Besides fixing funding models to meet the current threat, there are other policy efforts that can be undertaken to maximize the impact of existing cybersecurity resources. NASCIO believes the National Cyber Security Review, or NCSR, is an excellent opportunity to review our National preparedness and provide resources and technical assistance to fill gaps in our defenses.

The NCSR is a voluntary self-assessment survey designed to evaluate cybersecurity management within State, local, Tribal, and territorial governments. At the request of Congress, DHS has partnered with MS–ISAC, NASCIO, and the National Association of Counties (NACo) to develop and conduct the NCSR. The survey is now in the field and we expect final results to be provided in the first quarter of next year. Much like the Threat and Hazard Identification and Risk Assessment (THIRA) provides a guide for investment in traditional homeland security gaps, the NCSR could be followed up with the promise of Federal technical assistance to State and local participants who lag behind in vital areas. This will have the dual benefit of safeguarding citizen data and encouraging greater participation in National-level vulnerability assessments.

NASCIO also supports efforts to include State governments as a participant in programs that build the public sector cybersecurity workforce. One of the greatest difficulties States face is attracting and retaining talent in this information security sector. States cannot compete with the salaries provided by the private sector, or the allure of positions in the U.S. Federal intelligence services. Federal scholarships to study cybersecurity in exchange for working several years in the Federal Government, or for State or local governments, has the two-fold benefit of better protecting our citizens and expanding the available talent pool of cybersecurity experts. Scholarships should be expanded to ensure those who take advantage of them can work at any level of government protecting IT systems.

As many successful cyber attacks could be prevented by good cyber hygiene and security practices, Federal collaboration with State and local governments to create a culture of awareness and preparedness would also be a significant step forward. Just like "see something, say something," clicking one's seat belt before driving, or even covering your mouth when you sneeze, public awareness and habit is one simple way to significantly reduce the threat.

The Federal Government can also take steps to reduce burdens on State and local governments by harmonizing cybersecurity standards and requirements across Federal programs so State governments can provide more efficient and effective security of programs at a lower cost to taxpayers. Under the Federal Information Security Management Act, better known as FISMA, States are required to check certain boxes regarding security when taking Federal grant dollars. However, Federal agencies interpret these rules differently, and require different security standards. This often means that States must spend money on redundant systems to comply with a patchwork of Federal rules. It also means a lack of compatibility between various systems that States manage, which could otherwise be consolidated and more secure. Congress should work with NASCIO and the States to replace FISMA with cybersecurity rules that better conform to universal, outcome-based standards that would provide both Federal agencies and States with better security as well as greater efficiency.

Cybersecurity is a complex issue, and we have a long road ahead of us to making our Nation's systems more secure. There is no single solution here—or in tech speak, there isn't a "killer app." With the diffuse threat and diverse actors, cybersecurity requires a many-to-many approach. Most public safety response efforts are command-and-control, line-of-command efforts. Such efforts will not work when it comes to cybersecurity and response. With cyber attacks and the resultant impact, there is rarely a front line and the "path of the storm" is usually not obvious.

Holding hearings such as this one and finding ways to share information and resources will be crucial moving forward. We ask that Congress continue to work with the States in identifying ways to protect our Nation's digital assets, including rapidly maturing threat information-sharing entities and developing a common framework that can serve as a roadmap and provide funding justification for State cybersecurity. Thank you for the opportunity to testify and your time today.

Mrs. BROOKS. Thank you, Dr. Orgeron.

The Chairwoman now recognizes Mr. Sena for 5 minutes.

STATEMENT OF MIKE SENA, DIRECTOR, NORTHERN CALIFORNIA REGIONAL INTELLIGENCE CENTER, TESTIFYING ON BEHALF OF NATIONAL FUSION CENTER ASSOCIATION

Mr. SENA. Thank you, Chairman Brooks and Chairman Meehan and Members of the subcommittees. On behalf of the National Fusion Center Association I would like to thank you for the opportunity to share our perspective on this increasingly important issue.

Back in July the Majority staff of this committee released a report on the National Network of Fusion Centers after visiting more than 30 of them. The report noted that nearly 200 JTTF investigations have been created as a result of the information provided by fusion centers and nearly 300 terrorist watch list encounters reported through fusion centers enhanced existing terrorism cases.

Those successes were enabled because the National Network has developed into a mechanism for regular exchange of criminal intelligence and terrorism threat information across jurisdictions. This mechanism is ready made for information sharing on cyber threats as well, but we have a long way to go.

We need to recognize a couple of realities. First, a streamlined system of reporting, analyzing, and sharing threats and incidents requires leadership at the State and local level and the clear acceptance of what roles different partners can and should play. While the systems of interaction will vary from State to State, we need to structure relationships so that our personnel know where information should be flowing from and disseminated to.

Second, our human resource base at the State and local levels has not adapted quickly enough to address the increased cyber threats. State and local law enforcement, homeland security, and emergency management functions, including fusion centers, must have personnel who are adequately trained to respond quickly and share information rapidly so that additional crimes can be prevented.

The NFCA has been working over the past year with the International Association of Chiefs of Police, the program manager for the information-sharing environment, the Department of Homeland Security Office of Intelligence and Analysis, private-sector partners, and other associations to develop a pilot program. The pilot will be funded by the PM–ISE through DHS to the Center for Internet Securities, MS–ISAC.

The pilot will address needs identified by a wide range of stakeholders including the need for increased time lines, volume, and quality of information the Federal Government shares with State, local, and private-sector partners; the need for standardization of information-sharing processes among various levels of government; and the development of cyber response best practices; leveraging current counterterrorism tools and processes for cyber incident handling and intelligence sharing; and promoting private-sector cooperation and information sharing.

We expect the pilot to get underway soon and we look forward to updating the committee on our progress.

I want to raise four issues that we think this committee should be aware of and help us think through.

First, enhanced cooperation by Federal partners through more information sharing and Unclassified levels would help connect dots and lead to faster action. Our Federal partners tend to operate on the high side, but since threat information is coming into fusion centers from State, local, and private-sector customers who expect timely responses, operating in a classified environment can slow down information flow.

When the Classified document is created, an Unclassified version must also exist for dissemination. We need to get classification issue right so that we can be responsive to our communities while safeguarding critical infrastructure and key resources and information assets from exploitation.

Second, building training and maintaining a strong cyber analyst cadre within fusion centers and law enforcement should be a priority. We have great partners like the United States Secret Service, whose Hoover, Alabama facility provides cyber training for fusion centers and other analysts. That program should be a priority for new investment in the immediate future so that the training can reach a greatly expanded audience.

Third, the Terrorism Liaison Officer program is a successful partnership between fusion center and State and local law enforcement, fire service, first responder, public health, and private-sector communities within their areas of responsibility. This system maximizes situational awareness and provides a clear mechanism for ground-level suspicious and criminal activity to quickly funnel leads to investigative agencies.

The success of the TLO program in the physical domain should be extended to the cyber domain in the form of a cyber TLO program. Trained TLOs know what to do in the world of physical threats; the same should happen with cyber threats.

City, county, and State governments, as well as CIKR owners and operators should be part of the cyber liaison program. This mechanism would ensure that investigative leads filter up to the appropriate agencies while regular reporting on the latest cyber threats can be pushed down through the network.

Finally, every fusion center should have the ability to triage threat reports and develop products to help partners mitigate threats. Ideally, we need a constantly-updated automatic system that provides partners with the threat information—both machine- and human-readable—in real time, action to identify the attack, identify the associated indicators of compromise, and disseminate those indicators of compromise to partners in a timely manner. That is essential.

Thank you again for this opportunity to share our thoughts. I encourage you to continue to reach out to your fusion center in your State or region and find out about their challenges and best practices.

Thank you.

[The prepared statement of Mr. Sena follows:]

PREPARED STATEMENT OF MIKE SENA

OCTOBER 30, 2013

Chairman Brooks, Chairman Meehan, Members of the subcommittees, my name is Mike Sena and I am the director of the Northern California Regional Intelligence Center (NCRIC), which is the fusion center for the San Francisco Bay and Silicon Valley region. I currently serve as president of the National Fusion Center Association (NFCA). On behalf of the NFCA and our executive board, thank you for the opportunity to share our perspective on the analysis and sharing of information on threats from the cyber domain that we are seeing at a rapidly increasing pace.

The National Network of Fusion Centers (National Network) includes 78 designated State and major urban area fusion centers. Every center is owned and operated by a State or local government entity. The majority of operational funding for fusion centers comes from State or local sources, while Federal grants—primarily through the Homeland Security Grant Program at FEMA—are a major source of additional support. Our centers are focal points in the State, local, Tribal, and territorial (SLTT) environment for the receipt, analysis, gathering, and dissemination of threat-related information between the Federal Government, SLTT, and private-sector partners.

As the report on fusion centers that was released in July of this year by the Majority staff of the full House Homeland Security Committee noted, nearly 200 FBI Joint Terrorism Task Force investigations have been created as a result of information provided to the FBI through fusion centers in recent years, and nearly 300 Terrorist Watchlist encounters reported through fusion centers enhanced existing FBI terrorism cases. Most fusion centers are "all-crimes" centers, meaning that they do not focus on just terrorism-related threats. Most centers are supporting law enforcement and homeland security agencies in their States and regions through analysis and sharing of criminal intelligence to address organized criminal threats and to support intelligence-led policing.

Because the National Network of Fusion Centers has developed into a mechanism for regular exchange of criminal intelligence and threat information across jurisdictions, we are increasingly involved in addressing cyber threats. My center—the NCRIC—is actively involved in cyber threat analysis and information sharing with our Federal partners, other fusion centers, State and local governments in our region, and private-sector partners. As with any other successful law enforcement or intelligence effort, good relationships are at the heart of the matter. We must develop strong and trusting relationships with our customer agencies as well as with the private sector to ensure timely information flow. As an example of partnership development, the NCRIC is working with a major utilities service provider—that faces significant persistent cyber attacks—to assign personnel inside the fusion center. Once in place, this partnership will result in the development of capabilities to improve internal security for the company, but also new threat analysis and prevention capabilities for other critical infrastructure partners across the sector. The NCRIC hosts a working group including private-sector CIKR owners that meets regularly to discuss threats and share information.

But my center is not the norm across the National Network. Today, less than half of the fusion centers have a dedicated cyber program. We expect that number to grow as the threats grow, but we must have additional resources to support the specialized training and personnel to further that mission. We cannot take away from our established missions to tackle new ones. We also must coordinate closely with other entities that play roles in cyber threat awareness, analysis, and information sharing—including the organizations my fellow panelists here today represent.

The reality is that we are dealing with a growing category of criminal activity featuring different impacts as compared to traditional crime. Because the impacts are "quieter" and—to date—most often bloodless, it is more difficult to make a clear case for investments in systematic improvements in law enforcement and criminal intelligence capacity to deal with these threats.

But as we all know, the threats and their consequences are very real. And the threats are growing—from small, targeted operations that impact a family's finances to large operations that threaten an electric grid. Large critical infrastructure owners know who to call when something happens—they are likely to have existing partnerships with Federal law enforcement and investigative bodies. But who does a family call when they notice they have been violated? What about a small business or, even more concerning, a smaller vendor that may be part of an important supply chain? State and local law enforcement across the country are reporting increased calls related to cyber crime. Questions related to jurisdiction and investigative capacity are difficult to answer in many of these cases. But the analysis and sharing of threat information is essential to prevent more victimization.

As the NFCA has worked with our partners in State and local law enforcement on this issue over the past year, it has become clear that we have significant needs for capability and capacity enhancements. As I wrote in a blog post for the Program Manager for the Information Sharing Environment (PM–ISE) last week, the NFCA is working with the International Association of Chiefs of Police (IACP), the PM–ISE, private-sector partners, and other professional associations to assess needs across the country. I want to specifically acknowledge the office of the Program Manager for the Information Sharing Environment, DHS Intelligence & Analysis, and FEMA for their recognition of the importance of this effort, and for moving the ball downfield. These are outstanding partners in our efforts and we rely on them daily.

In August 2012, the NCRIC hosted a roundtable for cybersecurity stakeholders that included representatives from the financial and IT sectors, as well as Federal, State, and local officials. These participants identified two types of information sharing: (1) Fusion centers engaged in sharing tactical information on company or sector-specific situational awareness; and (2) fusion centers sharing strategic information on threats, risks, and trends through strategic forums that involve both the public and private sectors. IACP partnered with the Department of Homeland Security to facilitate a December 2012 roundtable to further clarify requirements for cybersecurity information sharing.

Building on the momentum of the August and December events, the NCRIC and the IACP held the Cybersecurity Evaluation Environment Pilot Kick-off Event in February 2013. The first day of this 2-day event focused on soliciting cybersecurity information-sharing requirements from industry partners and developing potential Federal, State, and local government processes for cybersecurity information sharing with the private sector. Participants also discussed Government requirements for cybersecurity information sharing. On the second day, the Government participants worked to design a "cybersecurity pilot" that would advance fusion center cybersecurity information-sharing capabilities.

The pilot will be funded by DHS through the Multi-State Information Sharing and Analysis Center (MS–ISAC) and executed in coordination with all appropriate stakeholders. It will focus on addressing needs identified by stakeholders including:
- the need for increasing the timeliness, volume, and the quality of the information the Federal Government shares with State/local/Tribal government and private-sector partners;
- the need for standardization of information-sharing processes between the Federal and State/local/Tribal governments and the development of cyber response best practices;
- leveraging current counterterrorism-developed tools and processes for cyber incident handling and intelligence sharing;
- enhancing the protection of State/local/Tribal networks;
- supporting cyber crime investigations; and
- promoting private-sector cooperation and information sharing.

We expect the pilot to get underway soon and we look forward to keeping the committee apprised of our actions.

We believe it is important to recognize a couple of realities. First, a streamlined system for reporting, analyzing, and sharing threats and incidents requires leadership at the State level in each of our States and a clear acceptance of what roles fusion centers can and should play. Roles, responsibilities, and capabilities should be clearly understood—including by private-sector partners—and we have to acknowledge that we are not where we need to be. That is why efforts like the pilot project we are about to engage in with the leadership of PM–ISE and IACP are so important. While the systems of interaction may vary from State to State, we need structured relationships so that our personnel know where information should be flowing from and disseminated to.

Second, our human resource base in investigative and intelligence settings at the State and local levels has not adapted quickly enough to address the increased cyber threat. Again, citizens report crimes to law enforcement no matter the type. Federal agencies cannot possibly investigate all of those crimes, even as they have a need to be aware of them in case they relate to other incidents in other locations. State and local law enforcement, homeland security, and emergency management functions—including fusion centers—must be resourced to respond to those crimes quickly and share information rapidly so that additional crimes can be prevented.

As the July, 2013 committee staff report on fusion centers noted, "Ultimately, it is the FBI's responsibility to conduct counterterrorism investigations. However, no single government entity has the mission and capacity to coordinate, gather, and look comprehensively across the massive volume of State and locally-owned crime data and SARs and connect those 'dots', particularly those related to local crime and, potentially, the nexus between those criminal activities and terrorist activity. This is the principal value proposition for the National Network." This reality extends to the cyber threat domain.

Next week the National Fusion Center Association will host a major event across the river in Alexandria, Virginia. The NFCA Annual Training Event will bring together fusion center directors and analysts from nearly all 78 centers, as well as Federal partners including DHS, partner associations from State and local law enforcement and emergency response, fire service representatives, and industry to receive training and share best practices. Among the training sessions are two separate sessions on cyber threat analysis and information sharing. Representatives from the Kanas City Terrorism Early Warning Group, the Orange County (CA) Intelligence Assessment Center, the Louisiana State Analytical and Fusion Exchange (LA–SAFE), the San Diego Law Enforcement Coordination Center, and my center—the NCRIC—will present to other fusion centers on effective practices and partnerships they are implementing in their centers. This indicates the level of interest across the National Network in advancing our capabilities to address cyber threats.

The State of Louisiana's fusion center—LA–SAFE—has taken an active role in cyber threat analysis and information sharing. State, local, and private entities reach out to LA–SAFE when a cyber event occurs in their AOR. The fusion center's lead cyber analyst disseminates block-list information to those partners to quickly help strengthen their protections. LA–SAFE conducts analysis of cyber threats and develops intelligence reports for dissemination to relevant partners. To date, the LA–SAFE Cyber Unit has developed more than 40 reports that have been shared with Federal, State, and local partners. Feedback to LA–SAFE—including from our Federal partners—clearly indicates that the information coming out of the fusion center is of high value.

In one example from earlier this year, the Louisiana State legislature was receiving numerous phone calls from a foreign individual asking for the payment of a supposed debt. The numerous malicious calls clogged the phone lines, preventing legitimate calls from going in or out. The "telephone denial-of-service attack" disrupted the legislature's communications. LA–SAFE determined that this TDOS attack was similar to others that had occurred across the United States and produced and disseminated an advisory to its partners. Immediately afterwards LA–SAFE received numerous phone calls and emails from public safety answering points (PSAPs) across the country that had suffered similar attacks. LA–SAFE was contacted by the deputy manager of the National Coordinating Center for Communications (NCC). The NCC had received the LA–SAFE advisory from the NCCIC and expressed serious concern. The NCC then initiated a conference call with LA–SAFE, the NCRIC, NCC, NCCIC, Association of Public-Safety Communications Officials (APCO), National Emergency Number Association (NENA), FBI, and other industry representatives to coordinate a response.

As a result of the coordination, multiple advisories were distributed from participating organizations to their customer bases. It has since been determined that over 200 of these attacks have been identified Nation-wide. These attacks have targeted various businesses and public entities, including the financial sector and other public emergency operations interests, such as air ambulance, ambulance, and hospital communications.

This example of cyber threat analysis and information sharing is occurring on a more frequent basis across the National Network of Fusion Centers. Some fusion centers are collecting and analyzing instances of cyber attacks in their AOR, and developing products that are sent to other fusion centers, which enables a much larger set of stakeholders to prevent damaging attacks.

LA–SAFE's recent experiences demonstrate both the opportunity and the need for additional focus and capacity within the network. Like other fusion centers that provide cyber threat analysis and sharing services, LA–SAFE needs more cyber analyst positions. The increasing threat level has already translated into increased demand for investigative and analytical services from fusion centers, and there is no sign of any slowing-down in that demand. A significant challenge for LA–SAFE and other centers is that cyber analysts are typically more expensive than traditional analysts. While physical terror threats and criminal activity are the primary focus of most fusion centers, the growing category of cyber crime means that cyber threat analysis resources must be strengthened at all levels of government.

In addition, LA–SAFE and other centers believe that the system for interacting with Federal partners on cyber threats needs to be improved. Enhanced cooperation by Federal partners through more information sharing at the Unclassified or Sensitive-But-Unclassified levels would help connect dots and lead to faster information sharing to prevent attacks. Our Federal partners tend to operate on the "high side," but since threat information is coming to fusion centers from State, local, and private-sector customers who expect timely responses, operating in a classified environment can slow down information flow. Speed is important in all investigations and prevention activities—especially in the cyber domain. We must work with our partners to identify the right path forward on classification so that we can be appropriately responsive to our communities while safeguarding CIKR and information assets from inappropriate exploitation.

Building, training, and maintaining a strong cyber analyst cadre within fusion centers and law-enforcement entities should be a priority. We have great partners like the United States Secret Service whose Hoover, Alabama training facility provides beginning and intermediate training for fusion center and other analysts. That program should be prioritized for new investment in the immediate future so that its training can reach a greatly expanded audience. The Multi-State Information Sharing and Analysis Center (MS–ISAC) provides training to State and local law enforcement to enhance cyber awareness and analytical capabilities. We need more of this type of training to ensure our analysts have the skills required to act quickly so that accurate, timely information can be shared broadly.

The Terrorism Liaison Officer (TLO) program is a successful partnership between fusion centers and the State and local law enforcement, first responder, public health, and private-sector communities within their AORs. TLO programs train thousands of individuals on indicators of possible terrorist activity and reinforce a system of reporting of suspicious activity through the fusion centers and the Nationwide Suspicious Activity Reporting (SAR) Initiative. This system maximizes situational awareness and provides a clear mechanism for ground-level suspicious activity to quickly funnel up to lead investigative agencies.

The success of the TLO program in the physical terrorism domain should be extended to the cyber domain in the form of a "cyber TLO" program. Trained TLOs know what to do in the world of physical threats. The same should happen with cyber threats. City governments, county governments, State governments, and CIKR owners and operators should be part of this network. Again, maximizing situational and threat awareness through a systematized reporting mechanism will ensure that investigative leads filter up to lead investigative agencies, while regular reporting on the latest cyber threats by fusion centers and other partners can be pushed down through that network.

Every fusion center should have the ability to triage threat reports and develop products to help State, local, and private-sector entities to mitigate the threats. Ideally, we need a constantly updated automated system that provides partners information—machine and human-readable—in real time as events are happening. Investigation into the source of cyber attacks will occur after the fact, but action to identify the attack, identify the associated indicators of compromise, and disseminate those indicators of compromise to partners in a timely manner is essential.

It will take time and money for that vision to be realized—and we have too little of both in the near term. In the mean time, the partners at this table and around the country must work together through the pilot project and other settings to develop policies, protocols, and requirements that will result in the kind of information sharing and threat analysis our citizens expect. In addition, a concept called analytical centers of excellence is being built out across the National Network. If a particular fusion center does not have dedicated cyber capabilities, then that center's personnel should know exactly where to go for support. Relationships should be developed and formalized so that centers with cyber capacity can be tapped when needed by other members of the National Network. This same concept is being applied to traditional criminal intelligence information by fusion centers today.

On behalf of the National Fusion Center Association, thank you again for the opportunity to testify today. The members of the NFCA executive board and I are happy to provide you with on-going input and answer any questions you have. I also encourage you to reach out to the fusion center in your State or region and find out about their particular challenges and best practices related to cyber and other threats. We look forward to working with you on this issue.

Mrs. BROOKS. Thank you, Mr. Sena.

The Chairwoman now recognizes Mr. Molitor for 5 minutes.

STATEMENT OF PAUL MOLITOR, ASSISTANT VICE PRESIDENT, NATIONAL ELECTRICAL MANUFACTURERS ASSOCIATION

Mr. MOLITOR. Thank you, Madam Chairwoman, Mr. Chairman, and the Ranking Members and all of the committee Members and staff who have joined us today. We would like to acknowledge the subcommittee for holding this important hearing on a very timely topic, which is cybersecurity and emergency management.

NEMA sees safe and reliable electric power as an enabler for first responders and supporting life-sustaining services like communications, food, fuel, and water in the event of a cyber attack. As we discuss the impacts of the cyber attack, direct parallels can be drawn to grid outages caused by natural disasters. Nothing shapes the discussion more than the lessons learned through the 2003 Northeastern blackout, the recent tsunami in Japan, the recent earthquake in Haiti, and the two events which affected the Congressional districts of many of the Members here today, Hurricanes Sandy and Katrina.

Large-scale outages are extremely disruptive to the health and well being of the affected population regardless of the cause. The question becomes: What are the most effective steps we can take to prepare for and mitigate this impact?

In much the same way as new information in communications technologies are reshaping how we work, learn, and stay in touch with one another, these same technologies are being applied to the electric grid, giving utilities new ways to manage the flow of power. Many people refer to this as the smart grid. This allows us to minimize the footprint of an outage, maintain power to critical facilities, identify those affected, shunt around downed power lines to increase public safety, and enable faster restoration of services.

Many of these technologies are detailed in a storm reconstruction guide that we produced in the wake of Hurricane Sandy a year ago, and we had a seminar on Capitol Hill earlier this year where we went through this in a fair amount of detail.

When the U.S. Department of Energy established their seven characteristics for smart grid in 2008 it included: Optimize asset utilization and operate efficiently; anticipate and respond to system disturbances—essentially, be self-healing; and also, operate resiliently against attack and natural disaster. The key to this kind of performance is rooted in consensus-based industry standards.

Standards define the interaction between entities to create both interoperability and cybersecurity. They allow electrical manufacturers to build security into the grid, which is preferable to installing free and open devices that are secured after installation. We want security built into the objects and not bolted on afterwards. Moreover, the standards-based monitoring features of the smart grid will facilitate communications between grid operators, emergency crews, and first responders.

The bill introduced by a Member of this committee, the SMART Grid Study Act, by Congressman Payne, would go a long way to evaluating the breadth and effectiveness of the solutions that have been deployed to date. Since 2009 we have invested billions of dollars in the smart grid, and if you want to improve something you need the measurement. We have been building; it is time to measure.

Additional considerations for the cyber future of the grid are contained in Executive Order 13636 and the National planning scenarios developed by the various sector-specific agencies of the Federal Government in conjunction with the Department of Homeland Security. Scenario 15 is entitled "Cyber Attack" and it provides a doomsday scenario for a pervasive attack on major elements of the Nation's communications infrastructure, weighing this scenario against the cybersecurity framework being developed by NIST under Executive Order 13636, the implementation of which is being supervised by DHS. This will give our industry an appropriate platform to ensure that we are as prepared as possible for an attack.

Finally, as a 20-year veteran of the U.S. Army and a former company commander and battalion operations officer I can say that it is one thing to have a plan but another thing to execute it. We should regularly conduct large-scale virtual exercises, like the National-level exercises in 2012, to test our response capabilities under the cyber attack scenario or the natural disaster planning scenario or a combination of the two. The greatest fear of our industry is that someone would launch a cyber attack in conjunction with a natural disaster, which would increase its impact.

The military performs these kind of exercises with great frequency and great success. It would be a good idea for us to figure out how we can structure regional, more detailed exercises under DHS for the civilian agencies and companies associated with the critical infrastructure, like the upcoming NERC event you mentioned earlier.

I want to thank the subcommittees for allowing us to testify today and I look forward to your questions and comments.

[The prepared statement of Mr. Molitor follows:]

PREPARED STATEMENT OF PAUL MOLITOR

OCTOBER 30, 2013

Chairmen Brooks and Meehan and Ranking Members Payne and Clarke, I thank you and the Members of the subcommittees for inviting me to testify today on cybersecurity and emergency management.

I am Paul Molitor, assistant vice president at the National Electrical Manufacturers Association (NEMA). NEMA is the association of electrical equipment and medical imaging manufacturers, founded in 1926 and headquartered in Arlington, Virginia. Its 400-plus member companies manufacture a diverse set of products including power transmission and distribution equipment, lighting systems, factory automation and control systems, and medical diagnostic imaging systems. The U.S.

electroindustry accounts for more than 7,000 manufacturing facilities, nearly 400,000 workers, and over $100 billion in total U.S. shipments.

On behalf of the 400-plus member companies of NEMA, I am responsible for all internal and external communications relating to NEMA's Smart Grid strategic initiative including interfacing with electrical utilities, manufacturers, State and Federal agencies, and the U.S. Congress. Prior to coming to NEMA, I had an established career in the communications industry building data networks in Top Secret environments and large, commercial public networks for the internet divisions of both BellSouth in the southeastern U.S. and globally for WorldCom. More recently, I spent time working with artificial intelligence systems in several Federal programs dealing with systems of systems, intelligence analysis, and National defense. Having this background has been a good fit for Smart Grid as we seek to bring additional communications and intelligence to the electric grid.

I was the first plenary secretary of the NIST Smart Grid Interoperability Panel (SGIP), founded the SGIP's International Task Force, participated in the cybersecurity committee, and served as the founding director for SGIP's industry-operated successor SGIP 2.0, Inc. I've also served as secretary of the U.S. Technical Advisory Groups for the International Electrotechnical Commission (IEC TAGs) for the Smart Grid strategy group (SG3) and the Smart Grid user interface committee (PC 118). I was named to the Canadian Task Force on Smart Grid Technologies and Standards (TF–SGTS) and serve on the Carnegie Mellon University Software Engineering Institute's Smart Grid Maturity Model (SGMM) stakeholder panel.

NEMA believes this hearing is incredibly important. Our Nation faces unprecedented cybersecurity threats that endanger not only our way of life, but our very health and safety as well.

One year ago Superstorm Sandy struck the eastern seaboard and had a devastating impact on so many lives and the economies of a wide swath of States. Sandy brought out the best in our first responders, emergency managers, Government officials, and everyday Americans.

The electric grid is essential to public health and welfare. So when Sandy knocked out power for millions of Americans, first responders, utility operators, and emergency managers sprung into action. Restoring power is part and parcel of emergency management.

Of course, it is not difficult to imagine a scenario in which the electric grid is shut down not by a natural disaster but instead, through a cyber attack.

Whatever the cause, resilient and reliable power is critical for first responders, communications, health care, transportation, financial systems, water and wastewater treatment, emergency food and shelter, and other vital services.

Much of our electric grid was built in the 20th Century but is facing 21st Century threats. New technologies are being manufactured and implemented today to transform the grid. When smart technologies are in place, power outages are avoided or minimized and lives, homes, and businesses are better protected.

THE SMART GRID'S ROLE

In much the same way as new information and communications technologies are reshaping how we work, learn, and stay in touch with one another, these same technologies are being applied to the electrical grid, giving utilities new ways to manage the flow of power.

A Smart Grid is an electrical transmission and distribution system that uses technologies like digital computing and communications to improve the performance of a grid, while enabling the features and applications that directly benefit the consumer.

A Smart Grid is not an all-or-nothing proposition; there are gradations of "smartness." As the electrical grid is modernized with advanced technologies, it becomes smarter. Given the diversity in electrical systems and the wide range of available Smart Grid technologies, there is no one method to measure the smartness of an electrical system. What matters is performance.

The basic operation of Smart Grid technologies is designed to give the utility company and the consumer (residential, commercial, and industrial) more control over the electricity supply.

On the consumer side, this means more information about—and thus greater control over—the charges that appear on individuals' electric bills.

For utility companies and other grid operators, this means acquiring better situational awareness to know what is happening on the grid and to better manage it.

By applying information and communications technologies and basic computing power to the electrical grid, utilities can not only minimize the footprint of an outage, but also identify those affected, shunt around downed power lines to increase public safety, and enable faster restoration of services.

For example, when disturbances are detected in the power flow, modern circuit breakers can automatically open or close to help isolate a fault. Much like a motorist using his GPS to find an alternate route around an accident, this equipment can automatically route power around the problem area allowing electricity to continue to flow to the customer.

Circuit breakers and other electrical devices in the field have the ability to communicate their status to help utilities identify potential problem areas, including outages or conditions that might result in an outage. Coupling this kind of automated activity with feedback from advanced electric meters would help restore service to the greatest number of customers even before the first truck rolls out of the utility service shop.

The Cyber Threat and the Electric Power Industry's Response

Like any infrastructure that is connected to a network, the electric grid faces cybersecurity threats which are increasing as each day goes by.

Protecting the Nation's electric grid and ensuring a reliable, affordable supply of power are the electric power industry's top priorities. Cybersecurity incidents have the potential to disrupt the flow of power to customers or reduce the reliability of the electric system. Key to the success of this effort is the ability to protect the grid's digital overlay against interruption, exploitation, compromise, or outright attack of cyber assets, whether through physical or cyber means, or a combination of the two.

The electric power industry takes cybersecurity threats very seriously. While new digital automation and technological advancements can introduce new vulnerabilities, these technologies also provide better situational awareness and help detect threats before an attack. As such, protecting the grid requires a collaborative effort among electric utility companies, the Federal Government, and the suppliers of critical electric grid systems and components—both hardware and software. Utilities are required to deliver affordable, reliable, and secure electricity, while manufacturers have an obligation to ensure that the same qualities are present in their equipment.

An infrastructure as massive as the electric grid which has been referred to as the world's largest machine cannot be simply taken out and replaced with the ultimate in cybersecurity. In other words, we cannot "gold plate" the entire electric grid, implementing the highest levels of security at every point along the distribution network. But a few techniques that have proven to be effective in sensitive operating environments in the Nation's Information Technology (IT) infrastructure will help ensure greater resiliency.

The first is segmentation. In order to control the cost of deployment, regulators need to consider the overall security architecture in their rulemaking decisions. As with the electric grid itself, the ability to isolate security issues and insulate core grid functionality from their effects is equally important as the strength of the security measure.

A second is layering. As with segmentation, the aspect of security layering needs to be considered during rulemaking. Individual security measures should not be considered in a vacuum, but rather in the context of how they contribute to the overall security architecture of the system. It would be important to define rules and guidelines for the levels of layered security required as a function of the criticality of a device, its functions, the impact on the surrounding segments of the grid, etc.

A third is decentralization. When we think about the computing environment of the 1960's, 70's, and 80's, it was dominated by mainframe systems and centralized control of information and processing. With the advent of the personal computer, this migrated to a much more decentralized model in the 1990's and beyond making access to computing resources much easier and more reliable for everyone. The same hold true with electricity as distributed generation, energy storage, microgrids, and net-zero energy designs and technologies become more available.

When an outage strikes, the effects often stretch far beyond the initial impact zone. Regional outages inhibit the ability to protect those in danger and provide basic needs such as food, sanitation, and shelter. We could recover more quickly if islands within each area could maintain power and serve as centers for critical services and recovery.

A microgrid can isolate itself via a utility branch circuit and coordinate generators in the area, rather than having each building operating independently of grid and using backup generators. Using only the generators necessary to support the loads at any given time ensures optimum use of all the fuel in the microgrid area.

Importance of Codes for Grid Resiliency

Of course, electric infrastructure isn't only transmission lines, substations, and transformers. It doesn't stop at the electric meter outside the building. Indeed, you could argue the grid extends to any end-use device you have plugged into an electrical outlet. Buildings consume some 70% of all energy produced and are the place where so much of modern life exists.

Emergency managers should recognize the importance of adopting the latest electrical code. The National Electrical Code (NEC) ensures that new construction and major renovations are built with the latest technology; which will make a facility as safe as possible for either those who become trapped in it during the emergency as well as the first responders who may have to breach the building envelope in order to stage a rescue operation. A robust emergency plan involves ensuring that updated codes are in place today to improve the outcome should disaster strike.

A corollary here is the energy efficiency of a building; energy codes establish baseline levels of efficiency. In the event of cyber attack, the best-prepared buildings will have a degree of back-up generation or may be part of a microgrid which is connected to some back-up generation. It stands to reason that a given amount of generation during the wider grid outage will be able to power more critical electrical loads or a given number of electrical loads for a longer period of time, as those loads' levels of energy efficiency are improved. In other words, energy efficiency allows us to do more with less during a grid outage.

NEMA is encouraging States and localities to stay current on code adoption.

Recent Congressional Activity

Some recent Congressional activity is worth noting.

Speaking of energy efficiency, Sen. Gillibrand has legislation which amends the Stafford Act to allow a recipient of assistance relating to a major disaster or emergency to use the assistance to replace or repair a damaged product or structure with an energy-efficient product or energy-efficient structure. When disaster strikes we should take the opportunity to prepare for future disasters by rebuilding the smart way, and energy efficiency is part of this, as described earlier.

Emergency managers and State and local officials are on the front lines for weeks after a major disaster. Often they are supported by the Federal Government in terms of resources, coordination, and manpower, but also in terms of funding to rebuild.

In the wake of Superstorm Sandy, NEMA encouraged Congress to allow Federal rebuilding funds to be used not only to replace damaged electrical equipment but to replace it with advanced technologies that allow the grid to become more resilient going forward.

The Senate version (H.R. 1, 112th Congress) of the Sandy Supplemental appropriations bill included the following language.

"SEC. 1105. Recipients of Federal funds dedicated to reconstruction efforts under this Act shall, to the greatest extent practicable, ensure that such reconstruction efforts maximize the utilization of technologies designed to mitigate future power outages, continue delivery of vital services and maintain the flow of power to facilities critical to public health, safety and welfare."

Unfortunately the bill that passed the House and was signed into law did not include such language. This approach should be considered in the any future disaster bill as a way to boost the resiliency of the electric system and ultimately lessen the impact of cybersecurity and other grid-impacting events.

Finally, on a much broader level, NEMA believes that Congressman Donald Payne's SMART Grid Study Act (H.R. 2962), which authorizes a study of the costs and benefits of developing a Smart Grid, would go a long way in proving the case—to those who remain unconvinced—that the Smart Grid is an investment worth making to make the electric grid stronger, safer, and more resilient. Investment in the Smart Grid is happening today across the country and around the world. Yet policy barriers remain to its full implementation.

A comprehensive study such as this, to be conducted by the National Research Council with input from the Department of Homeland Security and other relevant agencies, includes an in-depth review of the vulnerabilities of the electric grid to cyber attack.

THE IMPORTANCE OF INDUSTRY-LED STANDARDS

In addition to the obvious human toll a breach in cybersecurity could bring, from a manufacturers perspective it could involve countless hours of research and development staff time, contractors, and consultants, which would be a considerable financial burden on the utilities and manufacturers alike. The implementation of those patches would involve potential changes to the manufacturing process, deployment of patches to the installed base, product recalls, rebates and many other expensive options, not to mention the potential for lawsuits, both valid and frivolous, based on the potential outages described above.

An additional interest of the manufacturers is standardizing on common approaches to cybersecurity across utility areas of control as well as State boundaries. It is critical to invest the time and resources upfront to select the optimal architecture, minimize risks, and attain a reasonable balance between costs and security. Additionally, there exists a need for States to work together in order to provide utilities with a uniform security implementation approach. If public utility commissions do not lead with a common approach, then it will be very difficult for utility companies, manufacturers, the National Institute of Standards and Technology (NIST), and Standards Development Organizations (SDOs) to coordinate their security standards development efforts increasing the level of difficulty for manufacturers to provide interoperable solutions. The corresponding drop in interoperability could also lead to a lower quality of service to electricity customers.

The key to achieving the kinds of success described in this testimony is to rely on proven, industry-based standards. NEMA, along with a number of our NGO peers retains accreditation through the American National Standards Institute as a standards developing organization (SDO). Products made from consensus-based industry standards are the first step in achieving interoperability.

Smart Grid Interoperability Panel: Private-sector-led Voluntary Standards Processes for Cybersecurity

Because we live in an increasingly-connected world, interoperability has become a bedrock concept. The NIST effort through their Smart Grid Interoperability Panel (SGIP) focused on industry standards and their role in delivering the features and functionality for Smart Grid. Consensus-based standards ensure that devices achieve a minimum level of performance, whether that is in terms of safety or electricity delivery, with consistency and reliability. They also provide a uniform management information base (MIB) that allows operators to seamless trade management data to achieve successful operations in the segmented, layered, and distributed environment described above. Industry-based security standards further ensure that security measures can be properly vetted by the global security community. The practice of "security by obscurity", where security measures were individually developed and implemented without review, is not nearly as reliable as a publicly-tested and fully-vetted security scheme. Identifying cybersecurity standards through a body like NIST allows manufacturers to make sure that cybersecurity is built into the productions and solutions they offer rather than being bolted-on by the grid operator at installation.

NIST Cybersecurity Framework

The recently-released Executive Order for cybersecurity in the critical infrastructure (EO 13636) provides a template for the relationship between industry and Government. EO 13636, along with its predecessor legislation the National Technology Transfer and Advancement Act (NTTAA, Pub. L. 104–113) and its implementation through OMB Circular A–119 describe the role of Federal agencies for securely implementing information technologies in the Federal Government. Essentially these laws stipulate that the Government shall use industry standards to the greatest extent possible, vetted through NIST, and installed under the practices identified by the sector-specific Federal agency. The NIST framework developed under the guidance of EO 13636 adheres to this convention establishing an effective public-private partnership for the implementation of cybersecurity measures in critical infrastructure.

Incentives for Voluntary Participation in NIST Framework and/or Information Sharing

As we've seen in the information technology industry, information sharing about persistent electronic threats is a key component of security performance. When an electronic attack is in process, companies like Internet Security Systems and Dell SecureWorks detect and analyze those threats and provide that threat information to their customer base. The only way they can be successful in this is if their customers openly and willingly provide threat and attack information to them.

In order for threat analysis of critical infrastructure to be successful, electric utilities and others involved in the electricity supply chain need to be similarly forthcoming. This may mean that some form of inducement may be necessary in order to secure maximum participation. These don't necessarily need to come in the form of tax policy or direct financial incentives from the Federal Government, but something as simple as liability limitations for manufacturers and grid operators who have access to threat information that share it willingly with DHS or the appropriate sector-specific agency.

Privacy

NEMA member companies are dedicated to the protection of electricity subscriber privacy and personally identifiable information (PII). This is another area where consensus-based industry standards will play a role. Effective legislation or regulation regarding subscriber privacy needs to be based on common terminology and privacy concepts. This has previously been applied to other areas such as patient information in the administration simplification section of the Health Insurance Portability and Accountability Act (HIPAA, Pub. L. 104–191). Adaptations of these principles should apply to the electrical subscribers.

RESPONDING TO A CYBER EVENT

A front-line resource from the manufacturers of electrical equipment during any emergency is the NEMA Field Representative Program. NEMA field reps are building code and electricity subject matter experts. As experience masters in electrical systems, they have the kind of jack-of-all-trades knowledge necessary to deal with emergency situations. The NEMA field reps serve as a gateway to all 400-plus members of the association and can provide company- and product-specific advice as well as contacts within member companies who can help respond. The member company technical resources can then work with their utility company customers to safely restore power and ultimately repair the damage.

National Planning Scenarios Must Focus on Interoperability

DHS's work on the National Planning Scenarios gives them an appropriate entry point into the cybersecurity policy discussion. Scenario 15 of the National Planning Scenarios is titled "Cyber Attack" and includes the following General Description:

"This scenario illustrates that an organized attack by the Universal Adversary (UA) can disrupt a wide variety of internet-related services and undermine the Nation's confidence in the internet, leading to economic harm for the United States. In this scenario, the UA conducts cyber attacks against critical infrastructures reliant upon the internet by using a sophisticated C2 network built over a long period of time."

This, coupled with their role as defined in EO 13636 makes DHS the ideal place to host the analysis and evaluation of emergency preparedness testing for all elements of the critical infrastructure based on the current global threat profile.

NEMA has worked with DHS in this capacity in the past including a contract for the Digital Imaging for Communications in Security (DICOS) protocol associated with TSA electronic screening systems for airport operations. Two important features of DICOS are that it contains the appropriate protections for information privacy (being based on a corresponding medical imaging protocol named DICOM), and that an integrated threat model was part of the design consideration.

Essentially all of the tools and roles for DHS exist in other contexts, so the challenge will be to bring them together for the participation in cybersecurity event management. A future consideration should be a large-scale virtual exercise to test our response capabilities under the cyber-attack or natural disaster planning scenarios, or a combination of the two. The military performs this kind of exercise frequently with great success. It would be a good idea for us to figure out how we can structure a counterpart under DHS for the civilian agencies and companies associated with the critical infrastructure. Performed in real time, DHS can inject cyber events into the scenario exercise that would stress the communications and management capabilities of infrastructure service providers as well as Federal, State, and local agencies. The participants would then be compelled to respond to make sure they had the appropriate protections and contingency plans in place.

In closing, let me restate NEMA's commitment to improving the resiliency of the electric grid. We are willing partners with Government and industry in the effort to protect Americans from the threat of cyber attack and to help our country respond when disasters strike.

Mrs. BROOKS. Thank you, Mr. Molitor.

I now will recognize myself for 5 minutes of questions. Like to start out with Ms. Stempfley.

The After-Action Report for the National Level Exercise 2012 was released this summer. Can you please give us an update on the Office of Cybersecurity and Communications' efforts to work with other Federal agencies—specifically FEMA—as well as the State, local, and private-sector stakeholders to address the issues that were identified after this cyber exercise?

Ms. STEMPFLEY. Thank you, ma'am. Yes. Absolutely.

The National-Level Exercise was the first exercise where we had a cyber and physical scenario performed at this level. It was the attempt to bring together all of our stakeholders and look at how clear we had put roles, responsibilities, and execution and resources towards the specific problem. We were pleased to learn a number of lessons from that exercise, to include how to partner and the role the private sector must play in this very important mission area.

We have been undergoing a series of after-action activities, which range from the development of specific, more-focused exercises and action plans so that when a particular event might occur either in a sector or at a location we have playbooks available for that. These are being developed as a community, so not just DHS with FEMA but DHS with our stakeholder partners in the private sector, as well, with State and locals and other activities.

As a matter of fact, we worked with the energy sector to execute what we called the Poison Apple exercise not too long ago, which was one of these exercises testing a playbook of a particular scenario in the electric sector.

Mrs. BROOKS. Specifically, I am glad you bring up the electric sector, because as I mentioned, I just met with representatives from our energy sector just this last month and an issue that they brought up, which actually came up in a mark-up of bills yesterday, involved security clearances and the difficulty and the backlog in the issuance of security clearances for the private sector.

Can you please discuss that issue a bit and whether or not you are aware of the clearance backlog on the issuance process and are there anything that we can do to help you address—because it was my understanding from—and I had a number of private-sector companies that expressed that frustration, and it seems to me that if we are truly going to have this partnership, particularly with respect to a response, can you address this issue of security clearances?

Ms. STEMPFLEY. So one of the things that we all know and my colleague pointed out is we are not going to clear ourselves into solving these problems. So we are actively working on share lines and reducing information to FOUO and Unclassified activities. That is not to say that there are not times when clearances are required nor are we walking away or any of that from the security clearance issue.

My colleague, the assistant secretary for infrastructure protection, is very focused on this. Respectfully, I would like to take the question for the record and have her help——

Mrs. BROOKS. Who would that be?

Ms. STEMPFLEY. Caitlin Durkovich.

Mrs. BROOKS. Okay. Thank you. We would be very interested because it appears to be an issue that is causing a lot of concern in the private sector and we certainly respect the importance of security clearances but we must find a way to communicate and work together.

Ms. STEMPFLEY. Yes, ma'am.

Mrs. BROOKS. Thank you.

Like to ask Mr. Sena: When you talked about the fusion centers—and I have visited my fusion center and also would encourage others on the committees to visit their fusion center—yours is one of the small number of fusion centers in the National Network proactively incorporating cybersecurity into its mission, and I applaud you for that. What Federal, State, and local partnerships have you developed to help the NCRIC contribute to this important mission?

Mr. SENA. Thank you, Madam Chairwoman.

As far as the development of our fusion center capability—sorry. Thank you.

As far as our—still getting a little feedback here, but—the development of our center, we have been able to work closely with actually centers across the country to develop a cyber information network for exchanging information and then developing partners from the private sector to collaborate and actually provide them with timely information as well as working with our Federal partners from the FBI, from our partners in the Secret Services who are working the criminal angles of cyber threats, to be able to develop a network.

We are actually in the process right now of bringing in private-sector personnel to support that effort so that they are in an environment where we can share that information with them and develop products that they need. We have been working on that over the past year-and-a-half to develop a program and we are working right now to that National pilot to involve other centers and really develop centers of analytical excellence in the field of cybersecurity.

Mrs. BROOKS. Well, we look forward to you sharing that work with other fusion centers around the country.

I see that my time is expired and I am now going to recognize the gentleman from New Jersey, Mr. Payne, for any questions he might have.

Thank you.

Mr. PAYNE. Thank you, Chairwoman Brooks.

First I would like to thank Ms. Stempfley for discussing the New Jersey pilot project with critical infrastructure and emergency managers. I am very interested in learning, you know, about the pilot and hope that you can come back and discuss that with me at a later date.

Let's see. This question is for you, as well. Each witness here has discussed the urgent threat a cyber attack poses and that it is critical that the Government and the private sector take immediate action to beef up its cybersecurity efforts.

Earlier this month the Government was shut down for 16 days and I am interested in learning how that affected our cyber activities. Can you discuss how the Government shut-down affected cybersecurity efforts and which programs were furloughed and what projects were delayed as a result of that?

Ms. STEMPFLEY. Certainly the Government shut-down was a traumatic event for the staff in the Office of Cybersecurity and Communications. Important functions that were considered exempt associated with immediate loss of life or property were sustained during that period, including functions in the National Cybersecurity and Communications Integration Center, so our important information-sharing activities on threats that were on-going in that moment continued during this time frame.

Unfortunately, we had to suspend efforts in some other important activities, including workforce development, including outreach and awareness, and including engagement with many of our partnership and stakeholder engagement efforts. So all of our sector-coordinating council activities and planning activities were suspended during this time period.

Mr. PAYNE. Okay. So those are the programs that were furloughed?

Ms. STEMPFLEY. Yes, sir.

Mr. PAYNE. Okay. So how did it affect us in terms of our ability to thwart off these attacks?

Ms. STEMPFLEY. We focused during the furlough period on those efforts that were instantaneous or immediate—those monitoring of Government networks against threats and protection and defense measures about activities that were currently on-going. No progress was made during that period on programmatic activities and so future efforts nor planning activities occurred. So during this period we were required to focus exclusively on the near-term and real-time efforts of the Department.

Mr. PAYNE. So we could only focus on what was right before us at that time.

Ms. STEMPFLEY. Yes, sir. The requirement was we had to consider as exempt activities only things were about the immediate loss of life or property.

Mr. PAYNE. Would you consider us being more vulnerable at that time?

Ms. STEMPFLEY. It certainly was a time where there were not as many eyes on the Federal networks and it was a period where the vulnerability and the threat environment are something we are concerned about.

Mr. PAYNE. At our full capability do you feel there are enough eyes on it when we are at full deployment?

Ms. STEMPFLEY. I don't believe you will hear anyone from the Office of Cybersecurity and Communications acknowledge that the resources in this particular mission area are commiserate with the threat that we undergo, and so there certainly is more work to be done in that area. We have important programs, including continuous diagnostics and mitigation and the Einstein programs, which are a part of helping put automation into the Federal networks, and the Enhanced Cybersecurity Service, which is about helping to share information for protection with critical infrastructure.

Mr. PAYNE. Okay. Thank you.

Mr. Molitor, as you know, I have been a strong proponent of smart grid technology. Can you talk about how smart grid technology will improve resiliency in the event of a cyber incident?

Mr. MOLITOR. Yes, sir. Thank you.

The nature of a smart grid—and it comes from those performance objectives that were laid out by D.E., the whole idea that the grid should be able to react to disturbances and be somewhat self-healing. So the idea that if a cyber attack happens when the more intelligent grid than what we have today will be able to do is to be able to shunt around the areas that are affected. It doesn't matter whether that is an effect that is caused by a natural disaster, a man-made disaster, or a cyber attack.

So ideally what we want to do is contain the damage, and Madam Chairwoman this morning cited the television program this weekend, and that is an example of a cascading event, and what we really want to do is avoid that and that is what the technologies through the smart grid will enable.

Mr. PAYNE. Right. So in layman's terms, I, you know, was interested, you know, when you say you have a blackout at your home, you contact the utility, utility has to contact workers to go out to your home and start from that point and work their way back.

Mr. MOLITOR. Right.

Mr. PAYNE. What the smart grid technology would allow is almost for that affected area to contact the utility to say, "There is a problem in this area," which alleviates that working back and finding the issue and then figuring out what was wrong and then correcting it and getting it—so the smart grid technology would allow us to be proactive in protecting the grid and almost alerting us prior to the issue being created.

Mr. MOLITOR. Yes. Absolutely. The analogy that we have used in the past is like the dashboard on your car. You know, you have got the regular speedometer, tachometer, all of the things that tell you how the grid is functioning at the time.

But what we are really adding with the smart grid are the idiot lights—the things that come on when your oil pressure gets dangerously low and those kind of things. So yes, those are the automated notifications that can come off the grid and it can actually tell the emergency response crews in the utility companies where to go in order to fix and restore power to the greatest number of people.

There is a great example from Vermont Electric Cooperative, who was hit by Hurricane Irene in 2011 and then again by Hurricane Sandy in 2012. They had rebuilt smart in the interim period, and so they had a much easier time restoring service and they had much fewer consumers who were affected as a result of Hurricane Sandy than they were during Hurricane Irene. So we know that it works just exactly the way you described.

Mr. PAYNE. All right. Thank you.

Mrs. Chairman, I yield back.

Mr. MEEHAN [presiding]. I thank the gentleman from New Jersey and I want to thank each of the panelists for being here.

I am pleased to share the podium today with my colleagues from both sides of the aisle but particularly Mrs. Brooks. She and I served together as United States attorneys prior to our service in Congress, and as a result of that had the opportunity to work with a number of the fusion centers and others in the beginning of the process of creating what we hoped would be a robust capacity to respond to threats of terrorism both on the National as well as the local level.

One of the things that is eye-opening has been the tremendous success that has been realized in this country by virtue of, since September 11, we have been relatively free of the same kind of scope of a threat actually carrying itself out. But we have seen so many of the natures of the threats change, and I think this area of cyber is the one that probably creates, in my mind, the greatest concern. So there is a lot of effort that is going on and I am interested in hearing a little bit about your perspectives.

Let me start with you, Mr. Molitor, first. Just, you know, we have spent a great deal of time working here on cyber legislation, the purpose of which is to ease the ability for the private sector to communicate in a meaningful, two-way communication through the National—what we call the NCIC, the Cyber Information Center, with real-time information, and also the ability for you to be able to work it through in a way in which there are protections for sharing information and otherwise.

Have you had a chance to look at some of the proposed legislation and do you have any sense as to whether it would be beneficial to member companies like your companies within your organization and others similar across the country?

Mr. MOLITOR. Yes, absolutely. We are at the tip of the spear— the electrical manufacturers—in terms of cyber attacks. So when the attack comes in they are going after our members' gear as it sits in the electric grid. We need to be able to capture that information and then forward it, so that the folks at the fusion centers and the other panelists at this table can respond and react to it.

So it would be extremely helpful, just in terms of clearing the communications. During my opening testimony I mentioned something about how industry-based standards are the best way to do that. So we have to be able to communicate across multiple entities, between the electric utilities, between the Government agencies.

So yes, absolutely. It would be most helpful so that we know how to communicate with each other so we can standardize the messages and respond to the threat.

Mr. MEEHAN. Well, we are already dealing with it in real time, and I appreciate that. I think one of the realities is there is almost a triage, as you often do when you are dealing with an issue, and because of the threats that took place against the banking system and the, you know, in New York and other kinds of sort of major threats, the concern has been how we alleviate the potential for the drastic attack. But there is a lot of things that are going on that are impacting, as I think was well-articulated, State and local authorities who have a great deal of information, have a great deal of assets, are equally being probed, and otherwise.

So how are things working today with regard to the sharing of information? You have expressed some frustrations and some hopes, and I would like you to spend a little bit more time saying, well, suppose something happens right now.

Mr. English, Mr. Orgeron, and Mr. Sena, you are already, in various capacities, your fusion centers are working with some of the State and local organizations. Let us say you have an enterprise from another country—a criminal enterprise that is probing your data systems. How are you communicating today and what is it that allows you to work effectively together, or not?

Mr. ORGERON. Mr. Chairman, from a CIO perspective, I think that we are communicating with our fusion center. But one of the things that we have advocated is governance structures that are more clearly defined in terms of paths of communication.

The cyber component is, for all intents and purposes, is sort of the newer thing that we are adding into these threats, building into the processes that exist. So if there is an emergency management plan there should be a cyber annex to it in terms of key actors and what the roles those actors have——

Mr. MEEHAN. Are you telling me now that that is what your concern is, that that is not clearly identified right now?

Mr. ORGERON. I don't think that the governance is clearly identified across the States from a CIO perspective. That is certainly something, when we worked with NEMA and the National Governors Association in the cybersecurity call to action, that we certainly advocate. Governance was the top of the list in terms of paying close attention to authority and responsibility.

To your point about that, you know, what is happening at the State level, how those flows of communications are happening is something that we still think needs effort.

Mr. MEEHAN. What is your idea of a way to make it work?

Mr. ORGERON. I think you have to have a framework, and I think the framework has to be something that can be easily communicated in——

Mr. MEEHAN. What would it spell out?

Mr. ORGERON. Well, as an example, one of the things from a technology perspective is the NIST framework.

Mr. MEEHAN. Yes.

Mr. ORGERON. You know, a more common framework with which you can have a very effective conversation——

Mr. MEEHAN. Have you been following the meetings that have been taking place in California and other places and you are satisfied that they are working towards that direction?

Mr. ORGERON. It certainly seems so from the CIO perspective.

Mr. MEEHAN. Good. Good.

Mr. Sena.

Mr. SENA. Yes, sir.

Mr. Chairman, we do have an issue. You know, it took us a long time to get suspicious activity reporting worked out with a unified message, and there is currently a unified message task team working on the issue of cyber. But at the National level we have six different cyber centers and people are all saying, "Well, who do you call?"

Right now the message that is being developed, "Call any of them."

Mr. MEEHAN. Is this among your fusion centers—six of them are cyber centers, as well?

Mr. SENA. This is Nationally, at the Federal level—those different cyber centers that—and trying to work on who do you call?

Mr. MEEHAN. Who do you include as the National cyber centers? Because one of the parts of the legislation—and Ms. Stempfley's working very, very hard on this with DHS—is to create the NCIC as that central point, which everybody knows they go to one place.

Mr. SENA. Well, we have the NCIC and then there are investigative—National cyber investigative joint task force that is out there along with some of the other organizations that we have that have investigative responsibilities and agency responsibilities within their organizations.

Mr. MEEHAN. Who would you consider to be among them?

Mr. SENA. Within DHS, within FBI, within Secret Service——

Mr. MEEHAN. You are not trying to say there is any kind of jurisdictional issues going on among the Federal agencies——

Mr. SENA. Not at all. They are working very diligently together but it still causes confusion.

At the local level when you ask folks—when you go to an organization the companies that we have brought in said, "Who do you call?" and they go, "We have a rolodex of 100 people."

Mr. MEEHAN. Well, that is just counter to any kind of effective capacity to do things, isn't it?

Mr. SENA. Absolutely, sir. That is what we have been striving to do is to say, all right, let's create a unified message on where this information should go—and not just the telephone calls, but also the machine-readable information. This information moves quickly. The threat moves quickly. We have to respond to that as quickly.

Mr. MEEHAN. In fact, and I am—my time is up—but that is actually, in real time we do not have the ability, if we are responding to a threat which is happening in the cyber world, to rely on telephone calls to do it. It needs to be, in many ways, as they say in the old days, machine-to-machine to be able to mitigate these things, and oftentimes just identifying the nature of the threat, where it is emanating from and how we alleviate it in and of itself requires that kind of tremendous engagement.

Mr. SENA. Absolutely, sir.

Mr. MEEHAN. Well, I am grateful. That is a very, very good point. We are appreciative of your testimony today because this is exactly the kinds of things that we need to be able to look at to create that connection that works effectively, and that is something that we will work towards.

I am going to, appropriately, if you know anything about—Mrs. Brooks is going to take over the chairmanship of this hearing again. I am going to get back in my rightful place to her right.

So at this point in time I will return the chairmanship of the hearing to Mrs. Brooks and I thank you for your testimony.

Mrs. BROOKS [presiding]. Thank you, Chairman Meehan, for sitting for me while I quickly went to another hearing. This happens to us occasionally here as Members of Congress. We are called to other hearings that are also important and I actually may be called back because they were not ready for me. So we may be doing this musical chairs once again.

I now will, I believe, recognize the gentleman from Mississippi, Mr. Palazzo, for 5 minutes of questions. Thank you.

Mr. PALAZZO. Thank you, Madam Chairwoman.

Again, I want to thank the chairs for holding this joint hearing. I believe that cyber attacks could be as devastating as 9/11 and more widespread.

Just look at what happened a few weeks ago in Louisiana when the EBT card system went down for just a few hours. Widespread panic and confusion ensued. Just imagine what a cyber attack on our power grids or utilities would do to the stability of this Nation.

It is vital to America's interests to address our cybersecurity risks sooner rather than later. I think we must utilize all of our resources in preparing and responding to a cyber attack. It is not a matter of "if"; it is a matter of "when" that will happen.

I believe a good resource we could use is our Nation's National Guard. I am a proud original cosponsor of H.R. 1640, the Cyber Warrior Act. This bill establishes a cyber and computer network incident response team within the National Guard of every State and the District of Columbia, allowing the National Guard to assist in responding to cyber attacks.

It would also allow the Governor of the State to activate the incident response team to help train State and local law enforcement and other responders in cybersecurity and help them develop best practices. I am going to ask all the questions to weigh in on what they think of that bill and the utilization of the National Guard.

But before I do that I would like to ask Dr. Orgeron, could you speak to what Mississippi has done to prepare for a cyber attack?

Mr. ORGERON. Thank you, Congressman. Be happy to.

One of the things that we advocate at NASCIO and that we have done in Mississippi is risk assessment. So with the help of the Department of Homeland Security, in August of this year we had a tabletop exercise in our State. That tabletop brought in multiple agencies, our fusion center, and others to kind-of run through a scenario—multiple scenarios over about 2½ days.

It is in our document—in our call to action document that NASCIO worked with with NEMA and NGA. One of the things that is advocated is looking at what that risk portfolio looks like.

I will tell you that the outcome of that table-top really proved out some of the things that we have talked about here today—the fuzziness in some instances of understanding who needs to communicate with who, where those lines of authority and responsibility start and stop. We were very appreciative to the Department of Homeland Security for coming down to our great State and working with us and facilitating that process. We found it of great value.

It is one of the things that made its way into the call to action of States doing those kinds of exercises, so I certainly would advocate for that. I think the great State of Mississippi has benefited from it.

Mr. MEEHAN. Will the gentleman yield for 1 second on this?

Mr. Orgeron—

Mr. PALAZZO. Can you give me extra time towards—fantastic. I yield to the Chairwoman.

Mr. MEEHAN. I just cleared that with the Chair.

Did you do an After-Action Report after you——

Mr. ORGERON. I believe my chief security officer did, yes, sir.

Mr. MEEHAN. Would you make that available to us, please?

Mr. ORGERON. Of course.

Mr. MEEHAN. I would like that. Thank you.

Mr. PALAZZO. Dr. Orgeron, did the State CIOs typically have access to Top Secret security clearances to help protect their State from cyber attacks?

Mr. ORGERON. No, sir, typically not. It is my understanding that there are, I believe, two designated in each State—of course the

Governor, many times it is the director of homeland security or potentially public safety. NASCIO certainly advocates that, given the rise of the impact of cyber that the State CIO be considered if more clearances were going to be allocated.

Mr. PALAZZO. So you say States get two clearances?

Mr. ORGERON. That is my understanding, Congressman.

Mr. PALAZZO. Ms. Stempfley, would you like to add to that, and why they only receive two security clearances?

Ms. STEMPFLEY. Sir, I am not familiar with the limitation in that situation. I know we have actively worked to get clearances at the Secret level for State CIOs so that we can share the threat information, and generally that includes fulsome content for protection measures. So we have been actively working with NASCIO and others to get State CIOs cleared at that Secret level.

Mr. PALAZZO. Well, I have been to the TS/SCI process and I know it is lengthy, but you don't want to cut corners because you do want to make sure we have the proper people accessing that information. So, of course, if we could lift any undue restrictions that would be nice so the States can be well prepared to access these threats.

If I may sneak in a question, you know, begin the utilization of the National Guard, the Cyber Warrior Act, if—I would just like if you all would want to share your thoughts? I will start with Mr. Molitor on the end, a fellow soldier.

Mr. MOLITOR. Yes, absolutely. I spent some time in the Wisconsin National Guard so I appreciate that. That is an ideal place. When I heard it earlier during the testimony I thought that is an ideal place to house that kind of capability because that State Governor can call on the National Guard for the response locally. That is where you bring together the civilian assets, the intelligence assets, and also the military assets to address natural disasters.

I was actually called out one time after a tornado in Wisconsin for recovery efforts, so it is the same kind of thing in my previous testimony, where the parallels between natural disasters and cyber attacks are—it is the same impact on the citizenry, and that would be a great place, I think, to house that kind of capability on each State.

Mr. PALAZZO. I definitely agree with you.

I guess we will keep going down anybody that wants to volunteer until the Chairwoman takes away my time.

Mrs. BROOKS. Important topic, so——

Mr. SENA. From the fusion center perspective, and also being a high-intensity drug trafficking area director in my center, we have had great support from the National Guard. They have been very good. That is the one thing that we are lacking—those folks that can go out there and help support, either through assessments or actually in reacting and responding to the threat issues.

Every day we are bleeding a million cuts from the cyber attacks. They are doing telephone denial of services combined with cyber attack on institutions and really cutting us to the core. They move much quicker than we can.

But having the Guard, having additional resources to deal with those threats is tremendous, so I appreciate that. Thank you, sir.

Mr. ORGERON. Same sentiment, Congressman. I know Chairwoman Brooks mentioned in the beginning, Maryland. Maryland is one of the States highlighted in document that has a relationship with our National Guard.

My own personal experience post-Hurricane Katrina was the formation of a wireless commission in our State, of which the National Guard had a seat at the table. We have built 144 towers across the State to communicate in the event of another disaster. That partnership has been wonderful for the States. I would certainly expect that this one would be equally as good.

Mr. ENGLISH. Congressman, we certainly support that in Georgia and our troops are readying for that mission as we speak. I would say, though, that we need to give consideration to it being a symbol, similar to the civil support teams and the homeland security response forces that are now known as a full-time effort on a daily basis that we can work with all the time versus a weekend-type assignment.

Mr. PALAZZO. That is a good point.

Ms. STEMPFLEY. We have heard this morning about the need for competent, skilled resources in the cyber environment. I know in the National Initiative for Cybersecurity Education we have really been focused on understanding the State and local needs in cybersecurity, as well. I understand the Defense Department and DHS and others are studying how to best apply these particular resources and these patriots to this problem.

Mr. PALAZZO. I want to thank our witnesses.

Madam Chairwoman, I yield back.

Mrs. BROOKS. Thank you. A very important point with respect to the National Guard and the critical role they could play and that they do play in many States.

I am going to start on our second round of questioning, and if I—and this is to Mr. English. As I mentioned in my opening statement, you know, I did watch that movie that aired—not certain if others did—the "American Blackout," this past weekend, and it really did portray the physical consequences of a cyber attack on the electrical grid. One of the issues that was highlighted in that movie and that I actually had a discussion with folks in my district last week was the impact on hospitals.

As a leader in emergency management, I recently visited with representatives from a hospital, and as I was getting a tour of this hospital, and particularly in the emergency department, we began talking about if there were to be an incident of a cyber attack and its effect on a hospital system. While the physicians talked about the fact that, you know, they have operated, you know, until most recently without electronic medical records and could certainly perform their duties, what they would have the most difficulty with were their diagnostic equipment—the imaging technology and all of the ability to get all of the diagnostics that they now are so accustomed to receiving in real time, very, very fast turnaround, whether it is test results or lab results.

So I am curious from the emergency manager's perspective and the cybersecurity professionals, how do you coordinate with hospital systems and has there been a focus on that beyond making sure they have back-up generators and the fuel? What kind of coordination are we really doing with our hospitals? Because I have to tell you, this emergency department, while it has been discussed,

I think they acknowledged and recognized that most have not really prepared for that possibility.

Any discussion on that, Mr. English?

Mr. ENGLISH. Yes, ma'am.

Whereas we can always do a lot more work—that is for sure—the NEMA, the association I represent, and the State public health directors have been, for the past 18 months, involved in a relationship where we meet at least twice a year with the leadership and discuss issues. Most recently, one of the issues that we are talking about are—is mission-ready packaging for hospitals so that in a disaster they have already quantified the type of assets that they need through our mutual aid compact that can go from one State to the next, or from a impacted area to a—or a non-impacted area to an impacted area.

So I feel like the relationship is good. I am thankful that throughout the past 10 years that States have been able to get more capability with the grant programs that have been available, and certainly a lot of those have gone toward hospitals and readiness and communication.

Now, the issue of the imaging and that type of thing, I am not familiar with that. But I do know that the dialogue exists.

Mrs. BROOKS. Well, and I—the hospitals certainly said they have done a tremendous amount of exercising on triaging and mass casualty events and so forth, but I think the possibility of truly a power—a significant and/or long-term power outage, I am just curious whether or not anyone else has discussed with their hospital systems this very potential possibility.

Anyone else have any discussions with their hospitals or with their public health officials about that possibility?

Mr. Molitor.

Mr. MOLITOR. Well, I haven't had those specific discussions but there was an article in a magazine about 2 years ago focusing on a hospital in Japan in the wake of the tsunami there, and they had a micro-grid in place, and so this goes to Mr. Payne's point about the smart grid. A micro-grid is a self-sustaining—it includes electricity generation and also management for the load so that you can fuel critical loads like imaging diagnostics during an outage.

So this whole idea of a micro-grid, a self-contained, powered administration unit within the hospital is a very real prospect. It exists today and there are hospitals, even in the wake of Hurricane Sandy, that were able to continuously operate in the middle of the rest of the area where the power was down because they had those kind of micro-grids, that smart grid technology in place.

Mrs. BROOKS. Do you have any idea roughly how many hospitals in our country might actually employ micro-grids?

Mr. MOLITOR. I do not, but we have a medical imaging division within my NEMA—you have got two NEMAs up here; get a little confusing.

Mrs. BROOKS. Sure.

Mr. MOLITOR. But we have a medical imaging division and I can certainly check with them to see if they have any data and report back.

Mrs. BROOKS. Okay. Thank you very much.

At this time I will ask Ranking Member Mr. Payne if he might have any further questions.

Mr. PAYNE. Thank you.

Let's see. Mr. English and Mr. Orgeron—I am sorry.

Mr. ORGERON. Orgeron.

Mr. PAYNE. Orgeron. I apologize.

Mr. ORGERON. That is okay.

Mr. PAYNE. In 2013, the National Preparedness Report, States reported to FEMA that the lack of funding to develop robust cybersecurity capabilities significantly contributed to the lack of confidence in State cybersecurity capabilities. Can you talk about the role of Homeland Security—the homeland security grant money in developing State cybersecurity programs and how reduced funding levels have affected the States' efforts to develop those cybersecurity capabilities?

Mr. ENGLISH. The lack of funding I don't think—or the cutback in funding hasn't impacted that situation, in my opinion. I think Mr. Orgeron mentioned earlier that maybe if the grant guidance was a little broader and could entertain a more robust effort in the cybersecurity realm would be what we would like to see. Not necessarily more money, but maybe flexibility within the money that we get to be able to build out the cybersecurity assets.

Currently in my State we do use grant money to provide cybersecurity analysts to our fusion center, but that is really a drop in the bucket on the financial side.

Mr. ORGERON. Mr. Payne, we would agree. I mean, I think our basic position is that the formulaic nature with the way the grants work, it may not be as appropriate in terms of the cyber threat, and we think some alterations there, much to Mr. English's point, would benefit programmatically as a whole cyber initiatives in States.

I should mention, too—it may be a good point to mention, too, that, I mean, the States are struggling with workforce issues as well. Not exactly related, but, you know, it is very difficult to recruit credentialed and excellent people.

There is, I have been told, in essence nearly zero unemployment in this sector. So, you know, we have a very difficult time in recruitment, as well, which can impact mission.

Mr. PAYNE. Okay. For you gentlemen, as well, with respect to the activities aimed at helping States prepare for, prevent, respond to, and mitigate the effect of cyber attack, what is the Federal Government doing well and what needs to be improved?

Mr. ENGLISH. I have got to sing the MS–ISAC praises. I think they are doing very well, and without great detail, had up-close and personal experience with their deployment to our State, along with our chief CIO—our CIO and the FBI and DHS and others. So I am more aware that that really worked well.

Mr. ORGERON. I agree. We have a great relationship with MS–ISAC.

Two other quick points: I mentioned our table-top cyber exercise that the Department—we got funding for, I think is a great, great tool at the State level to bring parties together to kind-of walk through, you know, exercises of various sorts. I think it is exceedingly beneficial to us.

Mr. PAYNE. The other end, what needs to be improved?

Speak now.

[Laughter.]

Mr. ENGLISH. I really don't have a lot of heartburn with what is going on in the coordination effort. I think we always want to make sure that States and local governments are included in the plans before they are made so that we can have input and that we are at the table. As I mentioned earlier, creating those reasons to collaborate I think go a long way.

Mr. PAYNE. So you say we are doing everything right?

Mr. ENGLISH. Out of ignorance, I would say yes.

Mr. PAYNE. Okay.

Mr. ORGERON. Well, you know, being the IT guy at the table, I think we want to be at the table when those conversations happen. I think it does vary from State to State on how those dialogues occur, but I think whether it is talking about the clearance issue or formulaic changes in grant programs, I think CIOs, or maybe even the chief security officers if not the CIO, certainly we would want them to be at the table during some of those dialogues, given the threats that we face.

Mr. PAYNE. Thank you.

Thank you, Mrs. Chairman. I yield back.

Mr. MEEHAN [presiding]. Thank you. I appreciate the gentleman from New Jersey exploring those areas.

Let me ask about the relationship that exists with the private sector, because one of the realities is 85 to 90 percent of the resources are really tied up in the private sector. We have heard numerous concerns about resources that are available, both with trained personnel and otherwise. Yet oftentimes—Mr. Molitor may be able to speak to—there are a lot of members of industries and others who have already made significant investment in individuals with skills who are there to—if we can share information appropriately—it also includes expertise.

What is your experience in terms of—Mr. Molitor, you can jump into this question but I am interested in those who are representing State or fusion centers—what is your experience in terms of working with the private sector and how you are taking advantage of any of their assets or information sharing in your local regions?

Mr. SENA. From my perspective I am probably the most blessed because my fusion center is in Silicon Valley area, so we have got some of the best technology companies in the world there. So we have got lots of resources and oftentimes they know better and more ways about dealing with a threat than we do in the Government or could ever think of.

So trying to, you know, bring them on-board to make them partners with what we are doing in the fusion center, so that way when they ask us a question we can provide them with an answer. If they have the answer we can share that answer with others.

They have, you know, bonded together over the last few decades in building Silicon Valley and the resources there, but the networks go well beyond there; they go across our country and across the world where they have, you know, resources. So trying to work closely with them, trying to give them those resources.

The question always comes up about the clearances, and even within the fusion center ourselves, it takes us a long time to get our own people clearances, so but also trying to get them up to speed and actually physically bringing them in so we can give them briefings and actually help them solve these problems together. That is my goal.

Mr. MEEHAN. So are there parts of your fusion center which include a regular seat from private industry as a member?

Mr. SENA. We have. In fact, one of our first folks that we brought in was from the health care industry. So right now we are working with some of our power partners and utility partners to bring them into the center to get them the backgrounds, to get them the resources they need.

Oftentimes some of these people already had worked in Government for one of the other, you know, organizations that dealt with cyber and now they are working for the private sector. So we are trying to use those resources they have to help us in our center.

Mr. MEEHAN. Mr. Orgeron, are you working at all with the individuals in the private sector in your capacity?

Mr. ORGERON. We do, Mr. Chairman. You know, States rely on telecom providers, big system integrators daily to get the work done in the States, so that reliance is absolutely there. I would expect not only in my State but in many of the States the need for dialogue and inclusion is imperative.

Mr. MEEHAN. Have you worked with CERT teams at all?

Mr. ORGERON. We have.

Mr. MEEHAN. Have they been helpful?

Mr. ORGERON. They have.

Mr. MEEHAN. Ms. Stempfley, Secretary, you have been a stalwart supporter of efforts to do some of these things, but one of the council recommendations from your own advisory council was taking advantage of some of the skilled alumni in DHS, among other things, and there was an idea of trying to do outreach to make some of them available. Has there been any progress made in the idea of looking for those who have been in service at DHS and are no longer there but are still able to lend a hand at times of crises?

Ms. STEMPFLEY. I regret, sir, I am not familiar with the recommendation that you speak of. But one of the things we work very closely with is keeping in touch with both former DHS colleagues and those individuals in the private sector who are a part of the owners and operator community of critical infrastructure, particularly those in the IT, communications, energy, electric, and other sectors.

I know you have been to our National Cybersecurity and Communications Integration Center, where we are very focused on integrating our private-sector partners into our operations activities and we work very closely with our private-sector partners in not just protection and planning efforts but in the response efforts, as well.

Mr. MEEHAN. Yes. This was a recommendation that was called the Cyber Reserve Program that was run through DHS, and it may or may not be implemented. I know what happens. There are a lot of good ideas that sound—they get laid on your plate in the midst of all of these, and I just wondered if you had any insight on that program.

Ms. STEMPFLEY. Thank you for making that connection in my brain. We actually post that set of recommendations. The then-deputy secretary established a task force to look at all of the recommendations from that Homeland Security Advisory Council—set of recommendations on workforce activities. We have moved forward on many of them. The cyber reserve efforts and the potential utilization of current and former DHS colleagues in execution of this mission is one that planning activity has been underway.

Mr. MEEHAN. All right. Well I thank you for that clarification.

My time is expired and I will turn to the gentleman from Nevada, Mr. Horsford.

Mr. HORSFORD. Thank you very much, Mr. Chairman, to you, to Chairwoman Brooks, to the Ranking Member Mr. Payne and Ranking Member Clarke, for holding this important and crucial hearing.

I want to commend my colleague, Mr. Payne, for his legislation on the study for the smart grid. I know in my State and in regions throughout the country we have heard time and time again about the need to protect critical infrastructure, including, you know, our electric grid and water systems and other things that play into the grid. So I look forward to working with you on that legislation and commend you and your leadership for bringing it forward.

After hearing the opening remarks I wanted to delve into a couple of questions that aren't on my prepared questions.

Mr. Sena, right?

Mr. SENA. Sena, sir.

Mr. HORSFORD. So I have been in my fusion center. I am from Las Vegas—40 million visitors a year, 2 million residents in Clark County, and sheriff took me on a tour, met with all of our emergency management, first responders—local, State, Federal, and private-sector participants at that fusion center.

What is troubling to me is you say all the right things operationally for what is needed—the integration, the sharing of information—but then we have policy that doesn't support that approach. For example, the UASI money. In my State, Las Vegas was eliminated from the top-tier funding communities for our fusion center and lost several million dollars. My hope is we will get that back and I am working with the Department and FEMA and other agencies to make the case, but the policy doesn't support the practice that you envision.

So I would like for you to touch on how funding like UASI is critical in supporting your needs, particularly with the cybersecurity focus, which, as far as I reviewed in the primary factors of the UASI money allocation, I didn't hear cybersecurity come up enough even though it is the most emerging threat to our critical infrastructure. So can you speak to that, please?

Mr. SENA. Absolutely, sir. Congressman, just to let—as you know, with the reductions in UASIs and the inconsistencies and how the funding goes for those grant projects to support fusion centers, fusion centers are owned and operated by State and local agencies. I myself work for the San Mateo County sheriff's office. But it is up to those regions how they develop those programs and some are highly dependent on Federal funding.

We have some fusion centers that totally support their operations based on their own State budgets, local budgets. But when we are trying to develop programs that have a National importance, that have—meet those National priorities, those National missions, we have to develop the funding stream to support those programs.

Basing it on—and UASIs have been great across the country, but if you have no money they have got no way to give anything to the fusion center, and therefore the fusion center cannot support their programs. That is where we are at right now.

The other issue we have is the grant time line cycle of 2 years now, which basically means that once you get through with all the management issues of trying to move funding you have about 8 months to spend your money. Well, most people's salaries go for 12 months. That creates a little bit of a problem.

But we have those huge issues between how the money gets to the fusion centers and how it gets devoted to those programs. Right now there is no consistency across the country in how that money is delved through. Not just in the case of the Las Vegas fusion center, but other fusion centers across the country that lost their UASI funding—to the point of some, 30 percent. How do you run an operation when you have lost 30 percent of your money or 100 percent?

Mr. HORSFORD. Right.

Mr. SENA. It is difficult.

Mr. HORSFORD. Well, it is difficult when you have these emerging threats, which are ever changing. Everything you all talked about today is, you know, the people we are trying to prevent from attacking us are more creative, more resourceful, are working around the clock, and yet we are not putting in the resources to combat that.

I think the UASI funding, Mr. Chairman, is one area that needs to still be reviewed and, you know, I am committed to doing my part in bringing forward solutions for how it needs to be reviewed. But I think the cybersecurity factor in how communities rank should be reevaluated. So I will put that on the table.

Mr. Chairman, can I have just 1 more minute?

Mr. MEEHAN. Yes. The Chairman will recognize the gentleman for a follow-up question.

Mr. HORSFORD. I just want to ask about this interrelation between State and Federal entities. Given the inherently interconnected nature of the cyber landscape, why is it that harmonizing standards for the Federal Government is beneficial but requiring the same of State governments which may interface with Federal systems is not? I wanted Mr. Orgeron to answer that question.

Mr. ORGERON. Sure. We talked about NIST earlier, and I think from a framework perspective we certainly think that having a common framework would be most beneficial, whether it is at the State level or the Federal level. Certainly a framework that would help the two entities communicate, you know, I think we believe would be a good thing.

Mr. HORSFORD. Thank you.

Mr. MEEHAN. I thank the gentleman.

The Ranking Member has a follow-up question and so I recognize the Ranking Member for——

Mr. PAYNE. Thank you, Mr. Chairman.

This was a question that Congresswoman Clarke had: Cybersecurity technologies have made a major advancement over the last decade, just as the IT industry has. But the electrical grid has been built over the course of 100 years.

So, Mr. Molitor, in terms of cybersecurity, how do we deal with the legacy equipment that was installed before anyone was thinking about cyber threats and what was to come and is here now?

Mr. MOLITOR. Yes. That is a great question. Fortunately, a lot of the legacy gear doesn't have the kind of communications capabilities that makes it hackable to begin with. But if you have got a dead zone in the middle where you don't have cybersecurity capabilities built in you have to build your cyber perimeter around it. So the objective is—and especially through these smart grid technologies—is that you have the communications ability and the sensing ability on the adjacent devices so that you can identify when that device in the middle starts to underperform. So that would be the best indication that you have.

The challenge that we have is that a lot of these assets that were installed in the electric grid have a 20-, 30-, or 40-year life span before they can be replaced by the utility companies. So, you know, part of the cure to this is being able to fix the accounting rules and the other financial rules so that they can depreciate those assets, get them out of the grid, and replace them with the ones that can respond properly to a cyber attack.

Mr. PAYNE. So in your opinion—and I will close with this and I will ask each of the witnesses—you know, the legislation I have introduced, the SMART Grid Study Act, do you think that is the direction we should go so we can understand what we need to do to ensure the critical infrastructure is cyber safe?

Mr. MOLITOR. Absolutely. I am a firm believer that if you want to improve something you need to measure it. You provide the mechanism to obtain that measurement.

Mr. PAYNE. Mr. Sena? Same question.

Mr. SENA. We definitely—I mean, for years we have been building a great castle with physical—sorry, sir—building a great castle with physical security issues, but we have got this moat around us that has a stream that goes right into our critical infrastructure and we are so vulnerable, but the resources are not going there. We do have to have that capability.

We do have to have better electronic resources to deal with threat in real time but we also need analysts and people that can accept the information and know what we are looking for. Right now that is our big problem, from the high-end technical side to the people who are operating the computers within the locations, whether it is Government, whether it is critical infrastructure, you know, spear fishing, opening up the wrong e-mail can open up your network to huge issues.

When it is considered to be the electrical grid or any of our other critical infrastructure, that can be our fall down. My goal is to prevent that as best we can, so thank you.

Mr. PAYNE. Mr. Orgeron.

Mr. ORGERON. I agree. I mean, State government, especially from a technology perspective, whether it is consolidated data centers or networks, are highly reliable on the grid, so absolutely.

Mr. PAYNE. Mr. English.

Mr. ENGLISH. Absolutely. We have to have the power to make things work, and thank you for doing that.

Mr. PAYNE. Okay.

Ms. Stempfley.

Ms. STEMPFLEY. So we certainly have talked about the linkages between the cyber and physical environment, and one of the things that we are focused on at DHS is helping as infrastructures are upgraded—as our aging infrastructure is upgraded and takes advantage of the technology that exists today, helping them understand how to be more resilient in this cyber environment. So I think that is an important focus area.

Mr. PAYNE. Well, I thank all of you witnesses.

Just for the record, this study would not cost any more money. The money is already in place and we have offsets that would take care of the cost of the study.

I yield back.

Mr. MEEHAN. I thank the gentleman.

I am just about prepared to gavel the hearing down but I have one question that I want to ask for those who are involved in the State side, because I know that there has been some discussion about the need we have for people who are capable of working with you in both understanding and then addressing these kinds of concerns, and then simultaneously we have got, year after year, students that are graduating from colleges and universities, junior colleges all throughout our country and they are looking for a job.

It stuns me that we have educational institutions on the one side that are already—not looking for grant programs; they are already taking tuition. Some of these kids are going into debt to do this, and then they come out and they are saying, "Where do I get my first job?"

Then here you are running organizations which are saying, "Boy, we need people in here." What are you doing even with your own State university systems to implement some kind of connection between the training that could take place and the availability of a workforce?

Mr. SENA. Sir, I have to mention—and thanks in great part to our partners in the Department of Homeland Security, MS–ISAC, and our other State organizations—we actually had a pilot, you know, internship program this summer—brought some of the most brilliant people into my center. Great employees, great interns. Did some tremendous work for us.

So we brought them in but, of course, we have no funding to pay for interns. We have no money to pay for, you know, those analysts. You know, eventually we are getting some money from our UASI to bring on some analytical staff, but, you know, we brought in eight interns who did great work and those interns across the country were also deployed—recruited by DHS, recruited through, you know, cyber exercises that they would do on the weekends to see who could, you know, do the best infiltration of systems.

So we had the best minds out there but we have no money to hire these people and that is—you know, that is the tragedy of it. You know, great interns and, you know, free labor force for us, but we need them long-term and there is just no sustainment for that right now.

Mr. MEEHAN. Do they get directed to private-sector opportunities?

Mr. SENA. We do. We give them, you know, pass their information along to the private sector. But as was said previously, you find very few open jobs in that sector. But right now it would be great if we had that ability even to pay the interns for the time they spend with us, but also to bring them into Government work. They are just—you know, from the State perspective, you know, money has always been tight, and especially nowadays it has been tight, so trying to have funding to bring in those brilliant minds is difficult.

Mrs. BROOKS. Would the Chairman yield one moment?

Mr. MEEHAN. Sure. Absolutely.

Mrs. BROOKS. I am curious, before others might respond, whether or not you are educating your governors, your mayors, your councils who appropriate the funds for your departments to understand what the cyber threat might be? Because obviously, you know, there is always a push for more police officers on the street, more fire fighters, but yet there needs to be—and when we may be calling them analysts is part of the problem in that they appear to be support staff when, in fact, they are a cyber force and can be like a street officer. How are you educating the executives and those, you know, with the appropriations authority to, you know, make sure that they understand what the needs are, just out of curiosity?

Mr. SENA. I can tell you that after we made a presentation to our UASI on what the threat was, it immediately voted to give us $400,000 right off the bat. So they see the threat. But that is only if they have the funding available to allocate, and in this case they had the funding.

That funding may not be there next year, but that is the problem we have. There has to be a funding source and currently most States don't have the funding source other than potentially through those Federal grants. Those, the allocation varies between those centers, like in Las Vegas, that they just don't have any money for it.

Mr. ORGERON. We certainly do advocate with the Governor, elected officials, the legislature, the importance of a topic like this and potentially the disconnect between really doing great Government and needing great people to do great Government that have the right skills, and this is a marked gap to the point.

To the other question, all the things Mr. Sena said—working with universities on co-op programs to get students in, internship programs. It is really at the local level—at the local-State level—I think more, you know, just that you can get them interested. I mean, States are doing phenomenal things across all kinds of projects, especially in our State with a new data center.

It tends to be keeping them is the thing. They are great kids, and so we do. We go to the universities regularly, go to recruiting fairs regularly, and so—and we will continue both of those things.

Mr. MEEHAN. Well, I want to say, I think on behalf of all of my colleagues here, we appreciate your service. In many ways you, as was articulated by one bit of testimony, are out of there on the tip of the spear, and the experiences that you have, as well, not only in what you are doing each day but by virtue of analyzing the nature of the threat and the challenges that we have, and then by taking the time to both prepare your testimony and be responsive to our questions helps us educate—helps you educate us to be your partners in working for better, more efficient, more effective ways to deal with what we all agree, I believe, is one of the great challenges that we face here and an emerging and ever-changing nature of the threat, different from, in many ways, from those which we have been addressing over the course of the recent decade.

So I thank the witnesses for your valuable testimony and the Members for their questions. The Members may have—from the subcommittee may have additional questions for the witnesses, and if they do we ask that you would take the time to respond in writing. We are certainly free for any further follow-up information you would like to forward to us for the record. We will keep the record open for 10 days for that purpose.

So without objection, the subcommittees stand adjourned. Thank you for your testimony.

[Whereupon, at 11:52 a.m., the subcommittees were adjourned.]

APPENDIX

QUESTIONS FROM CHAIRWOMAN SUSAN W. BROOKS FOR ROBERTA STEMPFLEY

Question 1a. FEMA has a number of incident annexes to the National Response Framework, including a Cyber Incident Annex. The current Cyber Incident Annex was developed in 2004, nearly 10 years ago, when technology and the cyber threat were very different.

The draft NCIRP states that it was developed in conjunction with the update of the Cyber Incident Annex. However, according to FEMA, the Annex has not yet been updated and will be not updated until later this fiscal year, with an anticipated completion in fiscal year 2015.

Will CS&C be involved in this update?

Answer. The Office of Cybersecurity and Communications (CS&C), working with a broad set of partners, to include the Federal Emergency Management Agency, will continue to advance the dialogue around coordinated planning through development of operational playbooks and other planning frameworks. We anticipate that CS&C would be deeply involved in any updates to the National Response Framework's Cyber Incident Annex.

Question 1b. In a broader sense, how do you work to coordinate cyber doctrine within the Department to ensure that the plans and procedures in place are up-to-date and applicable to the current threats we are facing?

Answer. CS&C works with the Department of Homeland Security (DHS) Headquarters and other DHS components on a continuous and on-going basis to coordinate cyber issues. Many of these interactions take place at the working level in order to keep pace with the dynamic cyber threat environment. There are weekly leadership meetings consisting of both internal DHS organizations as well as our interagency partners specifically to coordinate on cyber issues.

In November 2011, DHS completed the *Blueprint for a Secure Cyber Future: The Cybersecurity Strategy for the Homeland Security Enterprise* (Blueprint). The Blueprint provides a process to create a safe, secure, and resilient cyber environment for the homeland. The Blueprint identified capabilities necessary to achieve DHS's cybersecurity goals. The development of the Blueprint was truly a cross-organizational, integrated process that brought together elements of the following components and sub-components of DHS:

- DHS/NPPD Office of Strategy and Policy (S&P);
- DHS/PLCY Office of Strategy, Policy, Analysis, and Risk (SPAR);
- DHS/CFO Office of Program Analysis and Evaluation (PA&E);
- DHS/Office of Intelligence and Analysis;
- DHS/Office for Civil Rights and Civil Liberties (CRCL);
- DHS/Office of Operations Coordination and Planning (OPS);
- DHS/NPPD Office of Budget, Finance, and Acquisition;
- DHS/NPPD Office of Cybersecurity and Communications (CS&C);
- DHS/NPPD Office of Infrastructure Protection (IP);
- DHS/Science and Technology Directorate (S&T).

Accompanying the Blueprint is a Mission Management Plan that prioritizes the Blueprint capabilities that DHS will mature over the next several years. The Mission Management Plan serves as a baseline for coordination and assignment of tasks based upon the capabilities and responsibilities across the Department. An example of this would be leveraging the skills and resources of the U.S. Secret Service along with Immigrations and Customs Enforcement to investigate cyber criminals. The results of these efforts are used internally within DHS as well as a baseline for discussions with our partners across the interagency, State, local, Tribal, and territorial governments and the private sector.

Question 2a. In reviewing the National Cyber Incident Response Plan (NCIRP), I am a little unclear of the link and cooperation between the NCCIC and FEMA and have a couple questions regarding that link and cooperation.

Does FEMA currently have personnel that are stationed full-time at the NCCIC?

Answer. The Federal Emergency Management Agency (FEMA) does not currently have personnel who are stationed full-time at the National Cybersecurity and Communications Integration Center (NCCIC).

The DHS Office of Operations Coordination and Planning has a full-time employee stationed at the NCCIC and another full-time employee stationed at the FEMA National Response Coordination Center (NRCC). The National Operations Center (NOC) is also staffed by a full-time desk officer from the NCCIC and another full-time desk officer from the FEMA NRCC. This exchange of personnel facilitates real-time coordination and collaboration in the event of a cyber-related incident. The NOC, NCCIC, and NRCC continuously share information and have access to the DHS Common Operating Picture (COP) for situational awareness. Additionally, the NOC receives and integrates daily reporting from the NCCIC and the NRCC. Also, the three operations centers conduct coordination calls at least three times daily via the NOC's Operations Centers conference calls (NOC Blast Calls).

Question 2b. If "YES": Who is this person—from what office within FEMA? If "NO": Do you think it would be a good idea to have a FEMA representative at the NCCIC?

Answer. Recognizing the potential significance of a cyber-physical event and the value of close FEMA–NCCIC synchronization, staffs from the two organizations meet often to discuss planning and exercise activities and to maintain watch center-to-watch center communications. In response to Emergency Support Function–2 activations, NCCIC regularly deploys staff to FEMA operations centers. In the event of a significant cyber incident, FEMA would deploy appropriate staff to the NCCIC.

Question 2c. How does the NCCIC communicate with FEMA on the potential threats the NCCIC is seeing and their possible consequences that may require FEMA to respond?

Answer. NCCIC and FEMA communicate via watch center-to-watch center communications. FEMA receives NCCIC situational reports and awareness products, which highlight more significant cyber and communications incidents and the NCCIC receives FEMA situation reports on a recurring and routine basis.

The DHS NOC, NCCIC, and NRCC all have access to the DHS Common Operating Picture (COP) and Homeland Security Information Network (HSIN). The COP and HSIN are the primary systems used for sharing and viewing Unclassified information along with other situational awareness products. Also, all three operation centers participate in coordination calls at least three times daily via the NOC's Operation Centers conference calls (NOC Blast Calls).

Question 3. The draft National Cyber Incident Response Plan (NCIRP) states that it "was developed in close coordination with Federal, State, local, territorial, and private-sector partners." I am interested in hearing more about the Department's outreach process during the development of the NCIRP because we have heard from stakeholders that there wasn't sufficient outreach and that this is more of a "Federal plan" than a "National plan."

Answer. The Department of Homeland Security (DHS) developed the National Cyber Incident Response Plan (NCIRP) in close coordination with public and private-sector stakeholders. During the early stages of development, DHS asked for volunteers through the Cross-Sector Cyber Security Working Group (CSCSWG), which includes Federal and private-sector representatives from each of the critical infrastructure sectors and convenes under the auspices of the Critical Infrastructure Partnership Advisory Council. The Department also sought collaboration through intergovernmental partners, the information sharing and analysis organization community and among Federal interagency partners. DHS drafted the document by sending out discussion papers—generally draft sections of the NCIRP starting with scope and purpose—and captured notes from subsequent discussions with public and private-sector participants. In addition to incorporating review comments into iterative drafts of the NCIRP, DHS also held table-top exercises and the Cyber Storm III National Exercise to further inform versions of the draft plan. Among the participants in the table-top exercises were the Information Technology Information Sharing and Analysis Center (ISAC), the Communications ISAC, the Financial Services ISAC, and the Multi-State ISAC (MS–ISAC). The MS–ISAC includes among its membership the chief information security officers from each of the 50 States as well as several U.S. territories and local Government representatives. Cyber Storm III included participation from eight Cabinet-level departments, 13 States, 12 international partners, and 60 private-sector companies and coordination bodies. Together, these entities participated in the design, execution, and post-exercise analysis of the cyber exercise. Participation focused on the information technology, communications, energy (electric), chemical, and transportation critical infrastructure sectors and incorporated various levels of play from other critical infrastructure sectors. In addition, Cyber Storm III included the participation of States, localities, and coordination bodies, such as ISACs, and international governments to examine and strengthen collective cyber preparedness and response capabilities. During the exercise, the participant set included 1,725 Cyber Storm III-specific system users.

QUESTIONS FROM CHAIRWOMAN SUSAN W. BROOKS FOR CHARLEY ENGLISH

Question 1a. How are State officials responsible for cybersecurity and emergency management coordinating to ensure awareness of the cyber threats you face?

Answer. The type and scope of coordination occurring between State officials responsible for cybersecurity and emergency management officials vary widely by State. In a survey NEMA conducted in February 2013, we learned no clear best practice exists in assigning responsibility of coordination of resources to prepare for, respond to, or recovery from a cyber attack. Only 41.9 percent of States cited a specific director. Of the 41.9 percent, responsibility ranges from the emergency management officials to IT, homeland security, and the fusion center. Where those responsibilities diverge, coordination occurs much in the same way as it would with any other all-hazards risk.

Question 1b. What support are you getting from DHS in that regard?

Answer. Programmatic offices such as the Office of Cybersecurity and Communications (CS&C) within DHS continue admirable work in their outreach to State and local officials. The larger challenge however is that the overall DHS effort, to include agencies such as FEMA, must be comprehensive and coordinated in order to ensure all the nuances of the threat and impact of consequences receive appropriate attention. In recent years, as the issue of cybersecurity grows, agencies have a tendency to create niches within the Department instead of adopting a comprehensive approach. Without a cohesive strategy from the National level addressing the consequences of a cyber attack, we run the risk of being unprepared should an event occur.

Question 1c. What more could they be doing?

Answer. DHS must recognize the impacts of a cyber attack extend beyond public-private relationships or simply securing networks. To date, the Department offers little guidance on the potential depth and breadth of cyber consequences. A deeper analysis must be accomplished on current disaster-related statutes such as the Stafford Act to consider whether such attacks would be eligible for Federal assistance. If so, guidance must be provided to the States. If not, an on-going dialogue must occur so all interested parties understand the current limitations of State and local governments in these economically-constrained times.

Question 1d. Is there anything Congress can do to help?

Answer. As Congress considers legislative options, the needs of the State and locals ultimately responsible for the consequences of a cyber attack must be first and foremost. In May of last year, NEMA joined with nine other associations to ask Congress for your consideration of key principles and values when considering cybersecurity legislation. In addition to consideration of the principles and values, Congress must work with DHS ensuring all potential consequences of a cyber attack are thoroughly considered in appropriate authorities such as the Stafford Act.

Question 2. A movie titled "American Blackout" that aired in October portrayed the physical consequences of a cyber attack on the electrical grid. One of the major issues highlighted was the impact on hospitals.

I recently visited with representatives from a hospital in my district and we discussed cybersecurity. The doctors, particularly those from the emergency department, are extremely concerned with their ability to function in the event of a cyber attack that impacts their power supply. This goes beyond medical records. They are very concerned about access to imaging technology that saves lives.

In the event of a cyber incident that impacts the electric grid, how would emergency managers and cybersecurity professionals coordinate with each other and the private sector to determine how soon the problem could be fixed and in turn properly identify necessary resources to assist hospitals beyond the generators and fuel they regularly keep on hand?

Answer. We would typically treat this type of incident just as any other. Emergency managers operate in an all-hazard environment and would coordinate with the cybersecurity professionals as we would any other Emergency Support Function (ESF). The resources would be done the same way. There are many disasters that affect our power grid, from ice storms to major storm fronts. It takes a Federal-State coordinated approach to create and improve a threat-specific annex to State Emergency Operation Plans. Emergency management plans are intended to address impacts of all hazards, regardless of cause.

Question 3. States have repeatedly identified cybersecurity as the lowest core capability in their State preparedness reports. To your knowledge, when developing this assessment, were State chief information officers or chief information security officers involved in the process?

Answer. While the exact number is not known, the collaboration and inclusion between chief information officers and emergency management officials is increasing due to the threat and the increasing awareness of the issue. For example, in the State of Ohio, the State Security Information Officer was involved in the responses to cybersecurity in the State preparedness report. In Arkansas, the Chief Information Officers as well as the Chief Information Security Officers are involved in the process of identifying core capabilities.

QUESTIONS FROM CHAIRWOMAN SUSAN W. BROOKS FOR CRAIG ORGERON

Question 1a. How are State officials responsible for cybersecurity and emergency management coordinating to ensure awareness of the cyber threats you face?

Answer. Coordination on cybersecurity varies drastically from State to State. This has to do with different models of State governance and centers of authority for cybersecurity response and emergency management. This is not only reflective of the different maturities regarding readiness to respond to cyber threats in the States, but also the diverse topography of State governments. There is increasingly coordination between State CIOs with emergency managers and other agency officials regarding disaster continuity, recovery, and emergency management. As referred to in my testimony, NASCIO's 2013 State CIO Survey states:

"Not surprisingly, disaster recovery and business continuity are issues that continue to receive increased attention in the State CIO community . . . We asked CIOs how they approached these initiatives within their State. As Figure 13 shows, almost two-thirds of States pursue a federated strategy with responsibilities split between the CIO and State departments and agencies."

Figure 13

Please characterize the general approach to IT disaster recovery and business continuity in state government.

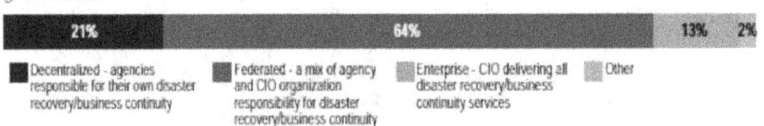

While our research shows increasing collaboration between State emergency managers and State CIOs, it is difficult to describe how a State would react to a cyber incident impacting a hospital as described in the question. The primary reason: With public-sector cybersecurity being such a nascent area, States have divergent governance and procedures in place to deal with significant attacks on critical infrastructure. Virtually every State has some means to provide support, whether through State police, its fusion center, or another State agency.

Further complicating matters, data does not exist to make extensive claims to best practices when it comes to governance. While several States have held cybersecurity exercises and learned from the experiences, the effectiveness of one governance model over another has not been thoroughly and publicly tested by real-world events.

Beyond this uncertainty, there are significant legal questions to be considered. For instance, a private hospital may not be able to take advantage of certain public resources. It is unclear a private entity could receive support from the National Guard without the declaration of a state of emergency by a Governor. Other questions come into play, as well: Legal liabilities, cyber forensics of a virtual crime scene, and more. The area simply has not been defined. The legal implications is an area that is ripe for Congress to explore.

Question 1b. What support are you getting from DHS in that regard?

Answer. There are several venues and tools from DHS or funded by DHS that provide State governments with additional awareness of and support in thwarting cyber threats. Perhaps the most prominent of these are the National Cybersecurity and Communications Integration Center (NCICC), United States Computer Emergency Readiness Team (US–CERT), and Multi-State Information Sharing and Analysis Center (MS–ISAC). Complementing and supporting State fusion centers and similar technical support is also of significant value as long as DHS ensures it is supporting the State's cybersecurity governance model. Broader efforts such as the National Initiative for Cybersecurity Education (NICE) are also vital for States to receive the type of talent they need to secure their systems, and should be expanded.

Question 1c. What more could they be doing?

Answer. In many States, neither Chief Information Officers nor their Chief Information Security Officers are cleared to the Top Secret level—only the Secret level. Therefore, they cannot receive vital information from the intelligence community on the most advanced international threats against our networks without explicit intention and additional pre-clearance. While DHS certainly would include a State CIO or his CISO in such a conversation, it is not so certain the rest of the intelligence community would know to reach out to the State CIO and clear them for such a briefing. This should be remedied.

NASCIO hopes that greater information sharing and better tools to disseminate this information will be released as part of the implementation of Executive Order 13636 and Presidential Policy Directive 21. NASCIO and its members are pleased with the on-going effort to provide greater declassification of cyber threat information as part of the EO, and look forward to seeing greater results.

In addition, we believe the National Cyber Security Review could be followed up with the promise of Federal technical assistance to State and local participants who lag behind in vital areas. This will have the dual benefit of safeguarding citizen data and encouraging greater participation in National level vulnerability assessments.

Efforts to provide support for cyber education among public employees in the States and broader social awareness of on-line threats, similar to public awareness campaigns in the vein of "see something, say something," are also valuable.

Question 1d. Is there anything Congress can do to help?

Answer. While opportunities for limited Federal assistance for cyber threats have been included in the National Preparedness Grant Program (NPGP), its shrinking pool of resources coupled with a formulaic structure that favors hardening targets against attacks at the jurisdictional level means States typically only have enough funding to maintain legacy homeland security investments and administer grants to local governments. For NPGP to meet the current threats faced by our States and localities, changes will need to be made to this program by Congress.

Greater resources for technical programs that support information sharing, technical assistance, and cyber threat exercises would be valuable, as well. Efforts to increase the public sector cyber workforce, ranging from targeted initiatives such as the DHS National Initiative for Cybersecurity Education to supporting computer science education in schools at every level, are extremely valuable. Such programs should be expanded and supported—both for the sake of our Nation's homeland security and our economic security. Larger public service campaigns to increase knowledge of the risks on-line, in the model of "see something, say something" or "click-it or ticket" would help reduce risk to both public and private-sector networks.

Question 2. As you may know, as a condition of receiving State Homeland Security Grant Program funding, the State Administrative Agency (SAA), which is usually either the State Homeland Security Advisor or Emergency Manager, must complete a Threat and Hazard Identification and Risk Assessment, which, as the name suggests, details threats and hazards facing each State. Some States, including my home State of Indiana, have included cybersecurity in their THIRAs.

To your knowledge, have your colleagues been included in this process to ensure the SAAs have the best picture of the cyber threats they face?

Answer. Unfortunately, NASCIO has no data on how many States include cybersecurity in their THIRAs, and whether SAAs have included their State CIOs in the THIRA process. NASCIO will to review this question with its membership and attempt to provide the committee with a well-researched answer in the near future.

QUESTIONS FROM CHAIRWOMAN SUSAN W. BROOKS FOR MIKE SENA

Question 1a. Your fusion center is one of a small number of fusion centers in the National Network proactively incorporating cybersecurity into its mission. I applaud you and your fusion center's efforts in this challenging environment.

What Federal, State, and local partnerships have you developed to help the NCRIC contribute to this important mission?

Answer. Response was not received at the time of publication.

Question 1b. What analytical products and situational awareness reports has the NCRIC produced? Do you have a sense as to how have these products been perceived by your partners?

Answer. Response was not received at the time of publication.

Question 1c. How is the National Fusion Center Association working to advance cybersecurity efforts across the National Network?

Answer. Response was not received at the time of publication.

QUESTION FROM CHAIRWOMAN SUSAN W. BROOKS FOR PAUL MOLITOR

Question. Mr. Molitor, in your testimony you mention the NEMA Field Representative Program.

Would you please tell us more about this program and how, if at all, these experts are available as a resource to emergency management officials during an emergency?

Answer. NEMA is the association of electrical equipment and medical imaging manufacturers, founded in 1926 and headquartered in Rosslyn, Virginia. Its 400-plus member companies manufacture a diverse set of products including power transmission and distribution equipment, lighting systems, factory automation and control systems, and medical diagnostic imaging systems. The U.S. electroindustry accounts for more than 7,000 manufacturing facilities, nearly 400,000 workers, and over $100 billion in total U.S. shipments.

The NEMA Field Representative Program is geared toward providing information and training to government officials (including building code officials, electrical inspectors, and emergency managers), maintaining the lines of communications between these individuals and the manufacturing community, and assisting in the wake of disasters. The relationships forged in advance of the disaster are invaluable in the ensuing confusion and turmoil. As advocates of safe electrical systems and installations, NEMA Field Representatives make a valuable contribution to public safety.

NEMA has four Field Representatives located in regional offices around the country. Their regions of coverage are aligned with the International Association of Electrical Inspectors (IAEI) Section Regions. The representatives are:

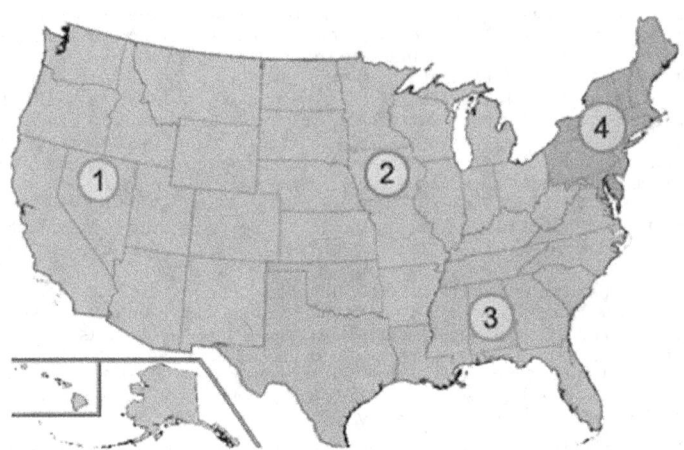

(1) Mike Stone.—Region: AK, AZ, CA, HI, ID, MT, NV, NM, OR, UT, WA.

(2) Donald Iverson.—Region: WY, CO, ND, SD, NE, KS, MN, IA, MO, AR, WI, IL, MI, IN, KY, OH, WV.

(3) Paul Abernathy.—Region: TX, OK, LA, MS, TN, AL, FL, GA, SC, NC, VA.

(4) Jack Lyons.—Region: ME, NH, VT, NY, MA, RI, CT, NJ, PA, MD, DE, DC.

PREPARING FOR EMERGENCIES

One of the most important functions of the field representatives is to support a 3-year adoption cycle by States and local jurisdictions for National model building codes—including electrical, life safety, and energy—to coincide with the 3-year National revision cycles. These codes are:

• NFPA 70 National Electrical Code;

- NFPA 101 Life Safety Code;
- NFPA 99 Health Care Facilities Code;
- NFPA 72 National Fire Alarm and Signaling Code;
- NFPA 720 Carbon Monoxide Detection Code;
- International Building Code (IBC);
- International Residential Code (IRC);
- International Energy Conservation Code (IECC);
- International Green Construction Code (IgCC);
- International Fire Code (IFC).

National model building codes provide the blueprint for constructing residential, commercial, and institutional buildings and other structures. They prescribe the minimum safety and performance standards which allow occupants to live and operate in a safe and optimally-performing building. Model building codes also prescribe the latest advancements in energy efficiency, resiliency in building structure, and life safety through the use of hazardous elements detection. The codes are revised through an open and transparent stakeholder process led by the International Code Council (ICC) and National Fire Protection Association (NFPA) every 3 years to incorporate advances in safety and technology in homes and buildings. Therefore, timely adoption in accordance with the National model revision schedule is vitally important.

Direct adoption and enforcement of the latest building codes every 3 years provides:

- enhanced safety to homeowners and building occupants through the use of the latest technology and knowledge in life safety (i.e., emergency lighting; fire, smoke, and carbon monoxide detection) and electrical hazard protection (i.e., arc fault circuit interrupters, ground fault circuit interrupters);
- utilization of the latest advancements in technology, enabling the use of on-site energy generation for back-up power and for ensuring the structural integrity of buildings.

Proper installation of electrical equipment is key to safety and resiliency. The NEMA Field Representative Program provides training to State and local code officials, inspectors, and installers on the latest codes and on the proper installation and use of NEMA member products.

RECOVERING FROM DISASTERS

While preparation is essential, loss of life and damage to property will inevitably occur. One responsibility of a NEMA Field Representative is to make himself available to Government officials after a natural disaster.

Because safety is of paramount importance to our member companies, all time, travel, and materials associated with the Field Representative Program is paid for by NEMA members. In years past, NEMA Field Representatives have visited areas destroyed by Hurricanes Irene, Katrina, and Sandy. They've also responded to both flood and snow emergencies in the Midwest, as well as the Colorado flood earlier this year. In January of 2010, NEMA offered its Field Representatives to assist in Haiti after its devastating earthquake.

When disaster strikes, NEMA promotes a number of resources for public officials addressing major infrastructure damage. NEMA's user-friendly *Evaluating Water-Damaged Electrical Equipment* [1] and *Evaluating Fire- and Heat-Damaged Electrical Equipment* guides are critical resources for protecting life and property after a disaster. Additionally, *Storm Reconstruction: Rebuild Smart* offers strategies for reconstructing electrical infrastructure in such a way that mitigates future disasters. All of these resources are available on NEMA's website, *www.nema.org.*

As rebuilding commences, NEMA Field Representatives assist in solving problems involving the installation of NEMA member products by serving as intermediaries between Government officials and NEMA member companies. Decision makers should involve NEMA in the wake of disasters and a recent example highlights this.

In the wake of Superstorm Sandy, the New Jersey Department of Consumer Affairs (DCA) issued a directive for installers. The DCA stated that for wiring that had been submerged under water, "If undamaged, no replacement is necessary." [2] This directive is at best unclear and the DCA implied on its web page the continued use of previously submerged wire is fine by stating that equipment was safe to use for 90 days.

---

[1] *http://www.nema.org/Standards/Pages/Evaluating-Water-Damaged-Electrical-Equipment.aspx#download.*

[2] *http://www.nj.gov/dca/divisions/codes/alerts/pdfs/hurricane_sandy_guidance_11_-2012.pdf.*

This position does not comport with the NEMA recommendations in *Evaluating Water-Damaged Electrical Equipment.*

The guide states:

"Electrical equipment exposed to water can be extremely hazardous if reenergized without performing a proper evaluation and taking necessary actions. Reductions in integrity of electrical equipment due to moisture can affect the ability of the equipment to perform its intended function. Damage to electrical equipment can also result from flood waters contaminated with chemicals, sewage, oil, and other debris, which will affect the integrity and performance of the equipment. Ocean water and salt spray can be particularly damaging due to the corrosive and conductive nature of the salt water residue.

" . . . .

"4.6 Wire, Cable and Flexible Cords When any wire or cable product is exposed to water, any metallic component (such as the conductor, metallic shield, or armor) is subject to corrosion that can damage the component itself and/or cause termination failures. If water remains in medium voltage cable, it could accelerate insulation deterioration, causing premature failure. Wire and cable listed for only dry locations may become a shock hazard when energized after being exposed to water.

"Any recommendations for reconditioning wire and cable in Section 1.0 are based on the assumption that the water contains no high concentrations of chemicals, oils, etc. If it is suspected that the water has unusual contaminants, such as may be found in some floodwater, the manufacturer should be consulted before any decision is made to continue using any wire or cable products."

NEMA Field Representatives expressed their objection to the DCA directive after it was issued, but NEMA's concerns were not addressed, and have yet to be. Subsequent to issuance of the directive, tragedy struck Seaside Park and Seaside Heights, New Jersey, when more than 50 businesses on the boardwalk were destroyed by fire. Investigators have ruled the fire accidental and believe electrical wiring that had been submerged by seawater during Superstorm Sandy is the culprit.

NEMA continues to advocate for electrical safety in New Jersey and across the country.

○

www.ingramcontent.com/pod-product-compliance
Lightning Source LLC
Chambersburg PA
CBHW081848280526
45789CB00007B/2616